5/7/97

Dear Mr Pangburn,
    Thank you for promoting
excellence in your students.
        Fort Plain Chapter
        N S D A R
        Deborah Shivington, Regent

THE BOOK OF
THE JUST

THE BOOK OF
THE JUST

The Unsung Heroes Who Rescued
Jews from Hitler

ERIC SILVER

Grove Press
New York

Published by Grove Press
A division of Grove Press, Inc.
841 Broadway
New York, NY 10003-4793

Library of Congress Cataloging-in-Publication Data

Silver, Eric.
    The book of the just : the unsung heroes who rescued
Jews from Hitler / Eric Silver.—1st ed.
        p.   cm.
    "First published in Great Britain in 1992 by George
Weidenfeld and Nicolson Limited, London"—T.p. verso
    Includes bibliographical references.
    ISBN 0-8021-1347-8 (acid-free paper)
    1. Righteous Gentiles in the Holocaust—Biography.
2. World War, 1939–1945—Jews—Rescue. I. Title.
D804.3.S585   1992   92-10075
940.53'18—dc20   CIP

Manufactured in the United States of America

Printed on acid-free paper

First American Edition 1992

1   3   5   7   9   10   8   6   4   2

In memory of Sidonie Brichta
and of my parents, Harry and Fanny Silver,
who gave her a haven
on the safer side of the English Channel

Contents

Illustrations

Pastor André Bettex, who shielded Jews in Le Chambon-sur-Lignon (© *Dinah Silver*)

Sempo Sugihara, the Japanese Consul in Kovno (*Yad Vashem archives*)

Aristides de Sousa Mendes, the Portuguese Consul-General in Bordeaux, with his wife Angelina (*Yad Vashem archives*)

Charles Coward, the 'Count of Auschwitz' (*Associated Press*)

Sara Rigler (Matuson) with five of the British prisoners of war who saved her life (© *G. Feinblatt/Media*)

The false identity papers of Tibor Berger (Shmuel Ben-Dov) supplied by Pastor Gabor Sztehlo (*by courtesy of Shmuel Ben-Dov*)

Archbishop Damaskinos with King George of the Hellenes on his return from exile (*Associated Press*)

Anna Borkowska receiving the Medal of the Righteous from the Israeli poet and former ghetto fighter, Abba Kovner, in Warsaw, 1984 (*by courtesy of the Kovner family*)

Zayneba Hardaga, flanked by her sister, Arifagic Nada, planting a sapling in Jerusalem, June 1985. On the right is Yosef Kabilio. (© *Isaac Harari*)

Selahattin Ulkumen, the Turkish Consul in Rhodes, at Yad Vashem, Jerusalem, June 1990 (© *Rahamim Israeli*)

The Albanian Muslims Vesel and Fatima Veseli with the Jewish families they sheltered in 1944 (*by courtesy of Gavra Mandil*)

Liberation Day, Tirana, November 1944 (*by courtesy of Gavra Mandil*)

Henryk Grabowski with Jewish resistance veterans in 1985 (*Moreshet Archives*)

Yvonne Nevejean, the saviour of many Belgian Jewish children, in Brussels, 1969 (© *Sylvain Brachfeld*)

The German Sergeant-Major, Hugo Armann, planting a tree in the Avenue of the Righteous at Yad Vashem in 1986 (© *Rahamim Israeli*)

The rubber stamp made by Moshe Bejski for Oskar Schindler in 1945 (*by courtesy of Judge Bejski*)

A railway document for Jews transported from Golleschau, a branch of Auschwitz (*Yad Vashem archives*)

Oskar Schindler in Cracow, 1942 (*Yad Vashem archives*)

Max Schmeling being proclaimed the winner after his sensational victory over Joe Louis in 1936 (*Associated Press*)

Maria von Maltzan, who sheltered Jews in her home in Berlin (*Ullstein Bilderdienst*)

'All that remained', a sculpture by Elsa Pollak in the museum at Yad Vashem, inspired by a display of victims' shoes at Auschwitz (© *Shevach Black*)

Acknowledgments

I am grateful to the following:

Dr Mordecai Paldiel and the staff of Yad Vashem, Jerusalem.

The *Jerusalem Post* archives and the indefatigable Ernie Meyer, who has covered the story of Jewish rescue for as long as I can remember.

The Moreshet archive at Kibbutz Givat Havivah.

Yehudit Wade, who helped with the research.

Sylvain Brachfeld and Yitzchak Kerem, who shared the fruits of their studies of Belgian and Greek Jewry respectively.

My friends and colleagues, Cordelia Edvardson, Richard Oestermann, Simonetta Della-Seta, Peter Philipp, Ephraim Lahav and Nadia Slovik, who helped with interviews, background and unfamiliar languages.

Lynn Sharon, for generously allowing me to draw on her late husband's unpublished memoirs.

Rescuers and rescued who gave me their time and their memories.

Judge Moshe Bejski, who read my typescript and saved me from avoidable errors.

Linda Osband, an ever-tactful editor for Weidenfeld & Nicolson.

My wife, Bridget, who once again saw me through the panic of authorship.

THE BOOK OF
THE JUST

Prologue

To Fight the Evil

'Israel gave me a medal,' a retired Polish foreign trade executive told me one evening in his Jerusalem hotel room. 'It said whoever saved one life, it was as if he had saved the whole world. I saved one life.' This book tells the stories of people who saved the lives of Jews, in quantities of one to 10,000, in a Europe where it was open season for their systematic or random slaughter. It is not a contribution to 'revisionist' history. The Holocaust happened. It was the product of a premeditated policy of extermination. It was the Nazis, not their detractors, who called it the 'Final Solution of the Jewish Problem'. The supreme obscenity of the last decade of the twentieth century is that anyone has to argue the case. Six million Jews died. If it was not precisely six million, it might as well have been. One million would have been atrocity enough. Ask the Armenians. The relics of the concentration camps are still there. The mass graves, the nameless ashes, the documents and the photographs cannot be willed away. I have too many friends with numbers on their arms. My mother's Austrian refugee housekeeper was the sole survivor of a family of thirteen Jewish brothers and sisters. Many of those who were rescued by the heroes of this book lost their nearest ones. As a reporter, I visited an Israeli counselling centre which is still putting together the pieces for survivors and their children half a century later.

The aim of this book is rather to show that there were people who cared, who were neither indifferent nor intimidated, who risked their own lives, liberty or careers to save Jews – and sometimes paid a heavy price. Hitler's Europe was not a world only of us and them, Jews and goyim, victims and victimizers. The tragedy is that there were not enough righteous ones. It was easier to look the other way, to safeguard yourself and your own family, or even – like the Polish 'friends' who murdered the parents of the future Israeli Prime Minister, Yitzhak Shamir, when they came begging for help – to join in the orgy of legalized bloodletting. But it is important that there were some who said 'No'. Important for those they

1

sheltered, important if the rest of the human race is to look itself in the eye.

No one can know how many there were. Scholars have estimated anything between 50,000 and 500,000, a range so wide as to be meaningless. The Jewish people, through Israel and the Yad Vashem memorial centre in Jerusalem, has honoured nearly 10,000 'righteous among the nations'. As time runs out and the borders of Eastern Europe open, dozens of witnesses are petitioning monthly for new names to be added to the roll. Few of the saviours sought or received recognition elsewhere. They talked reluctantly of their deeds. Their children often learned of them from others. For many, the post-war world was an anti-climax. Decades later, they remained painfully conscious of how little they had achieved, how much more would have been possible if other ordinary people had shown the same extraordinary courage, had dared to deny the prevailing barbarity.

'A few thousand righteous, a few million dead and a few hundred million Europeans – it all remains inconceivable in as much as one dares to think about it at all,' wrote the daughter of a Red Cross official who disregarded head office instructions and protected thousands of Hungarian Jews. 'Can we, the heirs of that generation, pass judgment – or can we only mourn? History proves that it was possible to fight the evil.'

Some who did fight it were patriotic Germans, officers and men in Hitler's own army, adventurers and industrialists, saints and sinners. Again, to say this is not to absolve the overwhelming mass of the German people. They elected the Führer to power with the racist *Mein Kampf* as his manifesto. They applauded his drive to dominate the world. After the adoption of the Final Solution as official policy at the Wannsee conference on 20 January 1942, they manned the death machine in the streets and the ghettos, the torture chambers and the camps. They were craven and, as many of these stories illustrate, corrupt. They could not even shelter behind a perverse idealism. 'For my generation there is no forgiveness,' said the sergeant-major who saved Jews working under his command in Belorussia, 'regardless of whether we were legally guilty or innocent. Anybody who wanted to see could see. Everybody knew the Jews weren't being shipped to paradise.' But here too, the fact that there were some Germans among the righteous made it possible to start again. An entire nation was not branded for eternity, though for Jews at least it remained on probation. My mother's housekeeper mourned in German in our English kitchen and consoled herself with the poems of Goethe, but she would never go back.

The protagonists of this book came from a score of countries in

2

occupied Europe, from France, Holland and Belgium in the west to Poland, Yugoslavia, Albania and the Soviet Union in the east, from Scandinavia to Greece and Italy. Some were British prisoners of war (one of these, Sergeant-Major Charles Coward, traded dead Jews for live in Auschwitz). A Japanese consul in Lithuania saved a *yeshivah* (a Talmudic seminary) of rabbis and students. Some rescuers were motivated by Christian charity, a few were Muslims. Formally or informally, many saved Jews as a contribution to resistance: they were perpetuating the struggle against the Reich. They were conservatives and Socialists, liberals and Communists. Some had a history of friendship for Jews, even of support for the establishment of a Jewish state in the Holy Land. Others had never seen a Jew before the war. All were testifying to a common humanity, to a collective and individual responsibility. A Bulgarian statesman, Dimo Kazasov, said, 'I do not believe that a nation that abandons its moral and human values has the right to exist.' The parents of Cornelia Schmalz-Jacobsen, a future Berlin senator, 'decided that it would be better for our children to have dead parents than a mother and father who were cowards'.

The more I dug into the archives, the more I realized that none of the well-known stories – the Dutch family who hid Anne Frank; Raoul Wallenberg, the Swedish diplomat who saved thousands of Hungarian Jews before being carried off to the oblivion of the gulag; Oskar Schindler, the German factory-owner immortalized in Thomas Keneally's award-winning novel, more fact as it happens than fiction – was unique. There were other families, other diplomats, other industrialists. Whole communities in Holland, France and Italy concealed Jewish fugitives. In the cases of Denmark and Bulgaria, it was as if the entire country was conspiring to frustrate the Nazi design. All but 472 of Denmark's 7,700 Jews were ferried across the sound to Sweden. About eighty per cent of Bulgarian and eighty-two per cent of Italian Jewry survived the war.

The narrative of this book follows the pattern of rescue, rather than its geographical distribution. There are chapters on communities which saved Jews, on Christians and Muslims, on resistance fighters and Germans, on prisoners and diplomats. Some stories qualified for more than one chapter. The communities were all devoutly Christian. The saga of the Danish fishing boats is told through the exploits of the German shipping attaché who sounded the alarm in time for the Jews to escape. It could have been placed under communities or Germans. I filed it with the diplomats. Conversely, the Turkish consul who shielded Sephardi Jews in Rhodes is included with his fellow Muslims.

I set out to write a book about heroes. In an unstructured way, I also found myself retracing the story of the Holocaust. Not the politics, not the

3

mathematics of genocide, but the daily degradation it imposed on its victims. Before consigning the Jews to the gas chambers or the firing squads, the Nazis stripped them of dignity. Perhaps they could not have butchered a people without first expunging its humanity. The testimony of rescued and rescuers is inlaid with humiliation. The anguish of the hunted and the separated. The constant fear of betrayal and execution. The slow horror of death in a cattle wagon shunted from station to station because a clerk had neglected to write its destination on the bill of lading. The shame of a middle-aged Berlin Jew begging on his knees for a priest half his age to shelter him in his church; or of a Lithuanian manufacturer's wife so frostbitten and starved on a death march that, in the words of her teenage daughter, 'She couldn't even pull down her pants any more.'

The Yad Vashem Holocaust memorial centre was the starting-point for most of my stories, but I did not restrict myself to rescuers awarded its medals and certificates. If you live in Israel and tell people you are working on a book about Gentiles who saved Jews during the Holocaust, you are constantly told, 'You must meet my brother-in-law. He has a fantastic tale to tell.' The Yad Vashem testimonies, and the adjudication committee's scrupulous assessments, were invaluable none the less. Where possible, I augmented them by interviewing rescuers and sur- vivors. I have not attempted to be comprehensive. With thousands of cases to choose from, that would not have been feasible, even if it were desirable. I have tried to tell a variety of good stories, some more familiar, some less. And through them to salute all those who saved a whole world by saving one life.

4

Conspirators of Goodness

Arnold Douwes, eighty-three and racked with arthritis, greeted me in flamboyant Hebrew on the upper floor of one of those steep, narrow Dutch houses. His old resistance partner, Max Leons, a retired Amsterdam insurance broker, had driven me to Utrecht to meet him on a chill, damp November day in 1989. 'He is a beautiful, fantastic man,' Leons, sixteen years his junior and still exulting with admiration, promised. I had first met Leons sixteen months earlier, when Israel honoured 120 Calvinist peasants from Nieuwlande, a cluster of obscure Delft-pottery villages, all canals and plank bridges, in Drenthe province in north-eastern Holland. They had sheltered 300–400 Dutch Jews from deportation and death between 1943 and 1945. In a phrase minted by Pierre Sauvage, a Californian film-maker, born in a similar community to Jewish refugee parents, they constituted a 'conspiracy of goodness'.

The Dutch villagers had earned the grove of 100 olive trees planted in their names beside the Avenue of the Righteous at Yad Vashem in the hills above Jerusalem. But it was Arnold Douwes and Max Leons, whom Douwes still called by his underground codename 'Nico', who gave them the opportunity – and cajoled and bullied them into taking it. Douwes, Leons and a patriotic local farmer-politician, Johannes Post, whom the Germans executed after forcing him to dig his own grave.

'I'm a black sheep,' Douwes said, smiling over soup and snacks served by a devoted niece. 'My father, grandfather and great-grandfather were ministers in the Dutch Reformed Church. I was born in 1906 in the village of Laag Keppel in Gelderland, north-eastern Holland. I was always thrown out of everything. They didn't want me. I was thrown out of two schools.' The high-spirited boy was expelled from his first school for stealing a 'No smoking' sign from a tram and screwing it to the desk of his headmaster, an inveterate pipe-smoker, and from his second for attaching another tramway sign, reading 'Seats seven', to a lavatory door. When he was also thrown out of an agricultural school, he tried his luck across the Atlantic. In 1936, Uncle Sam threw him out too:

'They thought I was a Communist, which I wasn't. But I stood up for the rights of the Negro. I went into a restaurant in Chicago. They always gave you a glass of water before you ordered anything. There was a Negro sitting alone, who didn't have a glass of water. I sat next to him and asked how long he had been sitting there. He said, "A long time, they don't want to see me." I asked the waiter why he hadn't served the man. He whispered, "We don't serve Niggers here." I raised my voice, told him he was wrong and cited the Constitution about all men being created equal before God. I told him, "You must serve this man before you serve me." The waiter went to the 'phone and called the police. The Negro had more sense than me. He went, I stayed. A squad car came. The waiter told them, "This foreigner is trying to tell us how to run our country." The police took me and gave me the third degree.'

After his release, Douwes bummed his way around the United States. While riding a freight train, he met a man known as 'The Professor', a leader of the Communist-affiliated International Labour Defence, an organization which fought for the rights of black Americans. 'If the Salvation Army had come,' Douwes insisted, 'I would have joined it, but the ILD came first. I joined the ILD because it was against discrimination.' As a 'red agitator', Douwes was thrown into Cook county jail along, as he put it, with murderers, rapists and thieves.

'The newspaper magnate William Randolph Hearst came to see me and offered me a cigarette. I refused to take it. "Never from you," I said. So he put a filthy piece in his paper about me. I was bailed out by a lawyer, Sidney Adler, who put up $2,000, but then they deported me through Ellis Island and I sailed on the *Hansa* to Bremerhaven.'

On his return to Holland, Douwes went back to his old agricultural school. The principal agreed to take him back and Douwes studied what was to become his life's passion, tree cultivation. After three years, he passed out top of his class, though the younger students called him 'grandfather'. He boasted that he had learned the names of 100 trees. After a brief spell working in France, he returned once more to Holland after the war broke out. Next, he found a job at a tree nursery near his old school at Boskoop. On 10 May 1940, he was woken by a man he was boarding with. 'How can you sleep?' he was asked. The air was full of 'planes. Douwes saw German paratroopers descending in civilian disguise. This was his baptism into both invasion and resistance:

'In Boskoop there were 800 nurseries, each one separated from the next by a small canal. Little bridges connected one piece of land with another. We took away all these bridges. Two men can lift one out. We made islands, hundreds of islands. The Germans fell in the water, or on the islands. They couldn't go anywhere.'

Dutch collaborators soon started looking for him, and his employer advised him to get away. He went back to Laag Keppel, where he found a job planting trees in a forest belonging to the local castle. The war soon caught up with him and furnished a first, unhappy apprenticeship in the rescue of Jews:

'There was a house there that was full of Jews who had fled from Germany, young boys and girls. They were training to go to Palestine. We talked a lot about what we could do. There was one Jewish family, that of Sam Jacobs the butcher, in our village. One day I was on a bicycle between two villages. A girl came running – I suppose she was Jewish – and said, "I have no more strength. Go to Sam Jacobs." I have never raced so fast on a bicycle, but I was too late. The Germans passed me as I crossed a little bridge over a river. I saw him taken away. He was sent to Mauthausen. Two weeks later a message came to the village hall: "The Jew, Sam Jacobs, is dead."

'Then I thought these German Jews have to get away. I went to the village policeman to listen to the news from London (radios were illegal for everyone except the police). I trusted him, but I found out that I was wrong. Nobody wanted the young Jews. I knew they had to go into hiding. I was working day and night, working alone, but I didn't get to first base. I hid one of the boys on a farm. The same village policeman fetched that boy and delivered him to the Germans. Then I was picked up by the German security police. They knew where to find me.'

Douwes was driven to Arnhem prison in a van with a forest ranger and his two sons. One of the sons had cut a cable feeding power to German searchlights. He was taken away and executed. The prison was still under Dutch control, and Douwes was soon released with a warning. He went underground, then fled the area when word reached him that the Germans had put him on a wanted list. He moved from place to place, to people he knew or their relatives. Eventually, he pitched up at the home of his sister's in-laws, three and a half miles from Nieuwlande, where he planted a garden of marigolds (orange was the colour of the Dutch royal family, and thus forbidden). Through his hosts, he came to know Johannes Post, a farmer and a conservative district councillor, then aged about thirty-seven, who was beginning to organize resistance:

'He believed one should never do anything the Germans wanted. I was the first fugitive in that village. Johannes didn't realize that the Jews were to be exterminated. At first, there were no Jews in Nieuwlande, but I had seen how Sam Jacobs had been picked up. Initially, Johannes needed identity cards for people who didn't want to go and work for the Germans.

'Through Johannes I got into rescuing Jews. My first job was to steal ID cards. One day there was a birthday party in Dedemsvaart, about twelve miles away. There were a lot of rather elegant women there, the wife of the mayor, women like that, who had left their coats and handbags in a corridor. I pinched almost all of the ID cards out of the handbags – about twenty at one time. They were changed by hand by a Jewish expert, Isaac Davids, known as Peter. The less you changed the better.

'Johannes began to realize what was happening to the Jews. Through a brother in the church, he established contacts in Amsterdam. It was Johannes who started the resistance in Nieuwlande. He had to go into hiding because the Germans were after him. He had already started placing Jews with local families. He had a very strong sense of what was right. He saw that innocent people were being persecuted. He would have done the same if they had been other persecuted people, not Jews. In a way, he had

8

been brought up to think of the Jews as the people of the Book, but I don't think that was a special factor in Nieuwlande. He hardly knew what a Jew was. He helped human beings.'

One of the first Jews Post helped was Max ('Nico') Leons, then twenty-one and unemployed. Leons had rosy, Dutch cheeks, a suspiciously Semitic nose and an appetite for adventure. After arriving in Nieuwlande from his home near The Hague in 1943, he adopted a new name and quickly taught himself to speak the local dialect. He found work as a farm hand, then joined Post and Douwes in the resistance.

After going underground, Post turned to armed resistance. 'Nico and I once met him in Amsterdam,' Douwes recalled. 'He had just robbed a bank and gave us money. Once he stole 80,000 ration card stamps.' Post came to grief when he tried to free one of his best friends, another resistance operative, from an Amsterdam prison. He trusted someone who was a Dutch SS agent and fell into a trap. The Germans arrested him and shot him. He was buried in Overdeen, near Haarlem, in what is now revered as a cemetery for heroes of the resistance. 'He blew into the people of Nieuwlande the spirit of resistance,' Douwes testified. 'That must never be forgotten.'

Before leaving Nieuwlande, Post had given Douwes a list of contacts and addresses of people who might be persuaded to shelter Jews. There were very few places in Nieuwlande where you could count on people day and night, Douwes found.

'Johannes briefed me, then went away. That was the beginning of Nieuwlande. Our work was to bring Jews there. We had several contacts in Amsterdam and other cities. There was Nel, Hennie and Winkel, one of our best contacts, and two students, Lennie and Piet. Nel and Hennie were not Jewish. Sometimes they sent Jews to us, sometimes we went to Amsterdam to fetch them. We would get the message in Nieuwlande, first by 'phone. Then, when there was no 'phone, the messages came to a man in a shop, who would call us in as we cycled past: "Two persons, Type A, B or C." Type A were the ones who looked most Jewish, Type B less Jewish, Type C not Jewish at all. Sometimes I was given a piece of torn paper. I had to present it to somebody in Amsterdam who had the other half. The pieces of paper had to fit. The Jews were in hiding, but there were no safe-houses in Amsterdam.

'One of the biggest problems was that parents and others taking care of children didn't want to let the kids go. They didn't realize the danger they were in. We lied to them, we lied to everybody. We said families would be able to stay together, and that there would be a good school for the children. Mostly we brought children, but also grown-ups. Amsterdam to Nieuwlande was about 125 kilometres. I tried to take trains with old-fashioned compartments and no corridor. I took first class because I thought it was less dangerous: there were not so many people. We went by the evening train if possible so that we travelled in the dark, but there was a night curfew. You had to be off the street by 8 p.m.'

On arrival in Nieuwlande, the resistance took pride in placing all comers. 'Everyone who was in trouble with the Germans, Jews or not Jews, got an address,' Leons explained. 'We always said "Yes". That's why we got into trouble. Our own people said we were too reckless, that we took too much hay on our fork.' Mostly they were lucky, but Douwes recalled more than one near disaster:

'Once I was bringing two sisters, aged five and seven. The train stopped in the middle of nowhere. It was dark. Inside too. The train was blacked out. We could hear people a van away from us. We thought there was bombing, or a check. It was quiet for a while, then the little girl, the five year old, in a corner, said, "I think the wheels came off." Everybody laughed. But nothing happened until we got to Hoogeveen, ten or twelve kilometres from Nieuwlande, where we usually got out. Nico was to meet us with two bikes. Instead, there were about 200 "green police" (Germans, the worst of the worst). I felt it in my bones. We got off on the wrong side of the train. One of the girls said, "This is the wrong side." I said, "Quiet!" We got away from the station. I put the two girls and their luggage over a fence, then jumped over myself. It was all dark. I could hear people shouting in German. I told the girls to stay behind a tree: "Don't move and don't talk." I went looking for Nico. I whistled and he whistled back. We got the bikes and made it to the baker's, our usual first stop in Nieuwlande.'

Dutch traitors were often more dangerous than the Germans. They spoke the same language, they knew the terrain, they knew the people. The resistance circulated their photographs. One of the most notorious was 'Johnny', a compulsive Jew-baiter. One night Douwes and Leons arrived at Ede-Wageningen station, which

served two towns, Ede and Wageningen. They were smuggling a
Type A Jewish girl from Amsterdam. The three of them set out to
walk with her suitcase from the station to Wageningen. They
hailed a passing taxi, Douwes recounted, but after a short while
they were flagged down.

'In the headlights we saw three people, two grown-ups and a
little boy in the uniform of the Hitler Youth. One of the men was
wearing a German SS uniform. The third was Johnny the traitor.
They stopped us. I wished I had a revolver. Good thing I didn't. It
turned out they weren't interested in us. They just wanted to take a
taxi to Wageningen. But there was not enough room for three of
them, only two. It with a capital "I" happened. The driver put the
lights on. Nico, a Type A Jew, had to cover his nose with a
handkerchief. I put my hands on my head to cast a shadow over
the girl. Then she said, "The little boy can sit on my knee." So the
boy, who was aged about ten or twelve, sat on her knee. That's the
way we went, with the Hitler Youth on the Jewish girl's knee and
Johnny the traitor in front. She knew exactly what she was doing.'

The next problem was to find shelter for the Jews in Nieuwlande.
At first Post's maid volunteered to help, but after three weeks she
had to admit defeat. The villagers were reluctant to take the risk.
They would give money, if they had it, but not a roof: hiding Jews
was punishable by death. Douwes would not take 'No' for an
answer. He knew the fate facing the Jews:

'So we lied, as we lied in Amsterdam. Otherwise we would not
have found hiding-places. We would say, "It's only for one night.
You can't leave them outside in the rain." Then we said, "Let's
make it two nights." Then, "Till the end of the war." If people said,
"We won't have one Jew," we brought them two. Sometimes we
gave them money. Not one of the villagers wanted to make money
out of it, but there were a lot of poor people. Some of the Jewish
parents paid very well. If the people who took the children were
well-to-do, we didn't pay them. We used the money to pay
somebody else.

'The main difficulty was that the villagers didn't want to do it.
There was a farmer. Very often he gave us money, but he never
wanted to take somebody into the house. We had a middle-aged
Jewish couple. We had told them that we had a wonderful place
and that they could stay together. It was all lies. We wanted to get

them out of Amsterdam. We brought them to the farmhouse in the centre of Nieuwlande. Above the door was written: "Except the Lord build the house, their labour is but lost that build it." We came and talked and talked. The two Jews were outside. The farmer had sworn he would not take one Jew. No, it was too dangerous. He said, "If you want money, I'll give you money." I said, "What's that you have over the door?" He opened the door and read it out. Nico said, "Thank you very much," swept the people into the house, dumped their bags and slammed the door. The farmer had no choice. He was a decent fellow. He couldn't put them out. The couple stayed a month till we found another place for them.'

One of the Jewish children they sheltered in Nieuwlande was Miriam Whartman, who now runs the consumer affairs department of the Histadrut labour federation in Jerusalem. Her father was a purser in the merchant navy. Her brother, six years her senior, had volunteered for the Dutch resistance. In June 1940, at the time Anne Frank's family went into hiding, Miriam was summoned with other fourteen- and fifteen-year-old Amsterdam Jewish girls ostensibly to work in Poland. Hundreds of girls went on that transport. Not one came back. They were taken straight to the Sobibor extermination camp. Miriam's mother refused to let her go. 'If they find us,' she said, 'we can't help it. But we're not just going.' So mother and daughter went underground, sometimes together, sometimes separately. Over the course of a year, Miriam stayed in twenty-three different places. Then, in the summer of 1943, they made contact with a student resistance group, who sent them by train to Hogeveen. They travelled alone with forged papers. At the station they were met by Douwes, who found them a bed for the night in Hogeveen, then ferried them to Nieuwlande. It was a strange, backward world for the city girl:

'Every village was rather small. There was lots of water. The whole countryside was criss-crossed with ditches, some wider, some smaller. The villages grew along these ditches, long and narrow. Usually there was a main street with a church, pastor living next to it, baker, postman, teacher. Behind it were the farms. To get to the farms you had to cross countless ditches. When people arrived in the dark, Nico and Arnold used to take them over plank bridges on bicycles. You had to get used to the bicycle in the middle of the night. Everything was blacked out. The fields were all of peat. People used it for heating and cooking. They were very poor.'

In Nieuwlande mother and daughter were separated. It was safer. They stayed apart for most of the next two years, but they wrote each other letters. After staying with a series of middle-class families, Miriam was taken to the home of a postman, Jan Dekker, while she was found somewhere more permanent.

'Suddenly I came into a very primitive house. There was no running water, the toilet was in an outhouse. They spoke a different dialect. It took me five days to understand what they were talking about. They had never seen a Jew before. They hated city people because city people looked down on them.'

From there Miriam moved to the home of the village baker, Bolwyn, whose family lived behind the shop. The Bolwyns had ten children of their own. The mother was an invalid, in bed most of the time. Miriam and the eldest girl, Hillie, used to do the housekeeping.

'There was no water in the house. I used to fetch water in a bucket from a well. The water was brown because of the peat. We had enough food for everyone, but I remember a lot of fleas. They didn't bother anyone but me. All the boys slept in two beds, all the girls in another two. I was the only Jewish girl with them. The family was very Calvinistic, very religious. That is the main reason why they saved Jews. They knew the Jews were the chosen people, and they had to be saved.'

That did not prevent them from trying to convert their charge to Christianity. Eventually, this prompted Miriam's mother, as strong-willed and down-to-earth as ever, to take her away from the baker's family.

'They said grace before every meal, then read from the Bible afterwards. On Sunday we'd go twice to church, morning and afternoon. Hillie and I, the two big sisters, had to check the younger children. Every child got a clean handkerchief, a peppermint and two or three cents to put in the collection. On Monday evenings they arranged lessons in the New Testament for me and other young Jews with the pastor. We went. It was lovely to go out, to visit a warm, civilized home, with cups of tea and books on the shelves. At home we could only read on Sunday evenings.

'Other evenings we mended socks. Big, thick woollen socks,

with holes worn by wooden clogs. You got used to it. Hillie and I had a lot of fun too. It wasn't all grim. On Monday we washed clothes all day. But even if we hadn't finished, I had to go to the pastor in the evening. All this talk about Jesus, reading the New Testament, got to me. I wrote to my mother: "I think if I believe in Jesus, I'll be a better Jewish girl." I'd been there eight or nine months at this time. It was the spring of 1944. Mother summoned Arnold and said, "Get my child away from there." Arnold took me away by train to Wageningen, near Arnhem, and placed me with a professor at the agricultural university. Afterwards Arnold told me how dangerous it was on the train. Arnold and Nico continued to take care of me.'

A few months later they took Miriam to stay with her mother in De Nieuwe Krim, a tiny village of about four houses near Nieuwlande. Two other Jews, a mother and son, were staying there with Jakob and Bonnie Hogeveen, who kept a grocery shop. They were a young couple with three small children. 'They were very poor people,' Miriam remembered, 'but they looked after the four of us. Their motive was only religion. The organization paid enough to cover the cost of our stay. They certainly didn't make any money out of us.' The Jews spent the whole summer of the Allied invasion and the following winter there, sleeping in a cellar. It was a dangerous time. There were so many Jews coming and going that, inevitably, the Germans heard about it. One evening rumours spread that the Germans were coming. A young neighbour, a resistance fighter, was shot dead in front of Miriam and her mother. They found weapons in his barn, but they did not find the Jews he was hiding.

Miriam's mother decided that the time had come to leave. One night they just walked out and went to another village, where they lodged with some old people. In the nearby town, they presented themselves as refugees bombed out of Arnhem. They were given substitute identity cards (Miriam became 'Carrie Peters'), which enabled them to move around with relative freedom until they were liberated by the Canadians in April 1945. 'I haven't been back to Nieuwlande,' Miriam told me in Jerusalem, 'but I know Hillie is still there. She took care of the widow and children of Johannes Post.'

In that perilous final year of Hitler's war, the Gestapo caught up with Arnold Douwes. It was October 1944. He was sleeping in a house where there were five Jews hidden beneath the floorboards. The woman of the house tried to wake him, urging him to flee to the forest, but after weeks on the run, sleeping in haystacks or hedgerows, he could not resist another five minutes in a cosy bed. 'I'm sure I could have escaped,' he insisted. 'They wouldn't have found me, but they would have found a lot of other things. They would have taken the householder into custody. They would have found the Jews. They would have found a black-market pig we had bought to feed them.'

First he was locked up in a local prison in Oosterhesselen, where he was caught trying to prise the bars off his cell window. Then he was transferred to Assen, the provincial capital, where he tried unsuccessfully to fake insanity. 'They wanted to know all sorts of things,' he said. 'I gave them a pack of lies. They wanted to know where Nico was. I didn't tell them. They knew a lot about both of us. Other people had told them. It was a miracle that it had lasted so long.'

On 11 December, the Germans were planning to execute seventeen underground fighters in Assen prison. Douwes believed that he was one of them. But before the firing squad could do its work, a resistance group mounted a surprise attack and rescued thirty-one of its comrades, including the seventeen condemned men. It was the closest of all close shaves. The rescuers had been ordered to abort the operation because their superiors thought that it would be too dangerous. In the event, the surprise was total and not a shot was fired.

After the war, Douwes married one of the Jewish girls he had rescued. They emigrated to South Africa, where their three daughters were born, and then to Israel. Douwes worked as a landscape gardener and on salt-water farming at an agricultural research centre in Rehovot, between Tel Aviv and Jerusalem. He reverted to his first love, growing trees on a *moshav* smallholding. He stayed in Israel for twenty-eight years and then went home to Holland in 1984 after his marriage broke up and he quarrelled with a son-in-law. But first Yad Vashem honoured him and Johannes Post. For once, the 'black sheep' was not thrown out.

• • •

A Jewish refugee arrived one day in the mountain resort of Le

Chambon-sur-Lignon in south-eastern France. He went from door to door seeking shelter from the German invaders and their Vichy French allies, but was afraid to admit that he was a Jew. For four days, the villagers turned him away. Eventually, he confessed that he was Jewish. Doors opened immediately. 'If only we'd known,' the householders said. 'Of course there's a room for you.' With slight variations, the story was told to me by two separate witnesses. One was a Jewish survivor, André Chouraqui. The other was a Protestant pastor, André Bettex. Between 1941 and 1945, the 5,000 inhabitants of Le Chambon and neighbouring villages on the Plateau du Velay in Haute-Loire conspired to shield between 2,500 and 5,000 Jews, among them the parents of Pierre Sauvage. Philip Hallie, an American professor of ethics who wrote a book about it in 1979, confided that the story of Le Chambon 'saved me from despair after I had spent years studying the cruelties in the concentration camps of Central Europe'.

Most of the Chambon people were austere Protestants whose Huguenot ancestors had fled there from Papist massacres in the late sixteenth century. Lesley Maber, an English teacher who lived in Le Chambon for forty-three years from 1939, wrote: 'The motivation of the plateau people is to be sought in their Huguenot descent, their Bible-based culture and their long history of persecution.' They felt an affinity for Jews who were being persecuted by the Germans, but their faith also bequeathed them a special obligation to the people of the Book. 'We were a self-contained community, living with and around the Bible,' explained Jean Lebrat, a ten-year-old schoolboy when rescue activity began in 1941 and now deputy mayor of Le Chambon. 'It came naturally,' added Roger May, whose family kept a hotel where most of the fugitives spent their first night after arriving at the local railway station. 'We had already taken in Spanish refugees fleeing Franco in 1936. Before that there were Armenians. Before that Huguenots.' A woman told Philip Hallie: 'What they were asking us to do was very much like what Protestants have done in France ever since the Reformation.'

Late one cold, wet Saturday night a Jewish woman with two little girls knocked on Pastor Bettex's door in Riou, three miles from Le Chambon. He took them in. The next morning he added a passage to his Sunday sermon in the Evangelical Free Church condemning the anti-Semitic policies of the Vichy administration and urging his congregation to help. A parishioner came up to him afterwards and said that he should have kept quiet. Now the Protestants would be a target. The Swiss-born pastor replied that God said you must not close the door to people in need. Almost half a century later, Bettex, now eighty-one, developed his theme:

'It was the biblical culture that we had been brought up to, an obligation to pray for the Jewish people. These are the children of Abraham, and God orders us to open the door to them. Many people remembered the persecution of the Huguenots. I remember from childhood that my father read the Old Testament as much as the New. This was our heritage. We didn't blame the Jews for the Crucifixion. It is all of us who killed Christ. It is not just a Jewish culpability. He died for the sins of all people.'

André Trocmé, the most celebrated and inspiring of the village pastors, wrote soon after his arrival in 1934:

The old Huguenot spirit is still alive. The humblest peasant house has its Bible and the father reads it every day. So these people, who do not read the papers but the scriptures, do not stand on the moving soil of opinion but on the rock of the word of God.

The pastors' biblical culture pervaded the plateau. You did not have to be either Protestant or devout, Jean Lebrat argued. 'About twenty per cent of the community at that time were Catholics,' he said. 'They didn't act differently. Some of them gave shelter to Jews.'

The plateau was in the part of France governed for the first half of the war by the puppet Vichy regime, rather than the Nazis. A German division was stationed not far away and German soldiers were sent to a Chambon hotel to convalesce. Vichy posted an inspector to command the local police. 'He wrote reports,' said Roger May, 'but he was never virulent in them.' Hitler's Final Solution was not a supreme priority in those parts. There were raids, none the less, German as well as French. The Vichy inspector, who was later assassinated by the resistance, searched Lebrat's home three times. The Gestapo arrested Daniel Trocmé, a nephew of the pastor, with three busloads of pupils from a boarding-school he ran for refugee children. They suspected Daniel, who spoke fluent German, of the crime of being a Jew. At 2 a.m. on 4 April 1944, they sent him to his death in the gas chambers of Maidanek. Lesley Maber was detained for four days in 1943. But for much of the time the threat of discovery was more latent than real. According to Miss Maber, 'No one knew what the consequences of hiding Jews might be. The sense of danger was always present, but we never spoke of it.'

Pastor Bettex said that, although the police never came to his home, there was always a risk: 'One evening a Polish couple called Lipowski arrived at a neighbour's house. They spent days with the neighbours, then there was a false alarm. The neighbours got a bit nervous and said that they couldn't stand it. The Lipowskis would have to leave. I don't judge them. We lived all the time with the fear of being caught.'

The strength of the Chambon conspiracy was that it was dispersed. In all, eleven pastors were involved. Refugees came because they had heard from friends that the plateau was safe, offering either a long-term haven or an escape route to neutral Switzerland. Some were sent by French or Jewish underground rescue organizations. Some of the refugee schools were funded by the American Quakers and other international groups. Magda Trocmé, the pastor's Italian wife, told Philip Hallie:

'If it had been an organization, it would not have worked. How can you have a big organization deciding on people who were streaming through houses? When the refugees were there, on your doorstep, in danger, there were decisions that had to be made then and there. Red tape would have kept us from saving many of them. Everybody was free to decide swiftly on his own.'

The plateau people were private and self-sufficient. They kept to themselves and they did not pry. Years later, they were surprised to find that a neighbour had sheltered Jews. They were unaware of doing anything heroic. 'I can't say how many I saved,' said Pastor Bettex dismissively. 'They came and stayed for a short time.' In fact, he sheltered a young woman, Simone, for two years. Jean Lebrat first said that his family had never sheltered Jews in the house, then added on reflection, 'Well, not for more than one night.' In the shadow of the Third Reich, people died for less. While researching his documentary about Chambon, *Weapons of the Spirit*, Pierre Sauvage asked an elderly peasant, who remembered him as a baby, why he had taken Jews under his roof. The man found the question puzzling. He could only mumble, 'When people came, if we could be of any help . . .' Lesley Maber, both an outsider and an insider, was convinced that the secret of their success lay in the silence of the plateau people:

'We all knew there were Jewish refugees, but no one knew if his neighbour was hiding any. In the farms the refugees remained invisible. I lived in Le Chambon from 1939 to 1982 and can assure you that we never spoke of what had happened before Hallie's visit. Then the reaction was – and still is – "Why all the fuss? It was only natural." The pastors, all deeply involved in the rescue work, were as discreet and silent as the peasants themselves.'

For all that, there were times when the Christian witness of saving Jews went recklessly public. Schoolchildren refused to honour the national flag each morning with a Fascist salute. During a visit to Le Chambon, the Vichy Minister for Youth Affairs, Georges Lamirand, was treated to a sermon on the text 'Thou shalt love thy neighbour as thyself', and high school students presented him with a letter condemning the forced deportation of Parisian Jews:

We feel obliged to tell you that there are among us a certain number of Jews. But we make no distinction between Jews and non-Jews. It is contrary to the Gospel teaching. If our comrades, whose only fault is to be born in another religion, receive the order to let themselves be deported, or even examined, they will disobey the orders received, and we will try to hide them as best we can.

When the local prefect warned André Trocmé that his men would soon come to investigate and declared that foreign Jews 'are not your brothers', the pastor retorted: 'We do not know what Jews are. We only know men.' During a round-up in the village square, Daniel Trocmé loudly accused a Vichy policeman of responsibility, then led the Chambonnais in a defiant song of farewell. However, the armed resistance, which was also active on the plateau, regarded the rescue network as a bunch of dangerous amateurs.

Another factor facilitating rescue in Le Chambon was that strangers were commonplace. The cool plateau was a summer resort. Le Chambon had hotels, pensions and boarding-schools. Refugees arriving at the railway station checked into the May family's fifteen-roomed hotel like any other guests. After one night, the pastors placed them on farms. 'People came to the hotel,' Roger May, then in his early twenties, remembered. 'We had a natural defence. This was a hotel. We didn't ask people to register. We put down the names of two or three people who were OK. The door was open to people who were not Jews. The more people we had, the less suspicious it looked.' By luck or design, the bar of the hotel was out of bounds to the German soldiers convalescing across the village square.

André Chouraqui, a young Algerian-born Jew, was studying at a *yeshivah* in the French town of Clermont Ferrand when the Germans invaded. The students were expelled in 1942. He went to work for an organization that saved children, especially those without parents. His job was to place them on farms. He spent three years on the plateau. In the summer of 1943, he evaded the Gestapo after being tipped off by Mme Andrée Philipp, an associate of Pastor Trocmé's, that they were looking for him. 'Not a single time while I was there did the Christians refuse to help us in every way possible,' he told me. Other survivors testify that no attempt was ever made to convert the Jews, who were assigned a room for religious services.

Pastor Trocmé was the dominant figure in the rescue operation, though some witnesses insist that he was not its only motor. Lesley Maber called him 'a remarkable man, an inspirer, but not an organizer'. He was no cartoon country priest. Born in Picardy in 1901, the son of a prosperous French Huguenot lace manufacturer and a German mother, Trocmé studied in Paris and at the Union Theological Seminary in New York, where he worked his way through college teaching French to the sons of John D. Rockefeller, Winthrop and David. His Italian wife, Magda, whom he met in a New York student cafeteria, was brought up as a Roman Catholic. What united them was social conscience, a determination to fight poverty and injustice. On returning to Europe, they worked among the urban poor in industrial northern France. Trocmé was at once a pacifist and a man with a towering temper. He was, as Philip Hallie put it, 'a spiritual and theoretical volcano, always producing new ways of conceiving things'. As a preacher, he was passionate and outspoken. His wife shared his commitment to the sanctity of life, not as a theoretical dogma but as a moral imperative, regardless of the risk. Their non-violence knew no borders. In the final months of the war, Trocmé preached against taking revenge on German troops captured by the resistance.

In a testimony to Yad Vashem in 1970, André Chouraqui wrote:

Pastor André Trocmé was the living soul and the spiritual personification of the French resistance. Through his personal actions, as an example to others by his demands and by his writings, Pastor André Trocmé undoubtedly saved – directly and indirectly – numerous Jewish souls, and helped to strengthen the spirit of the French resistance which, at the end of the day, contributed to the downfall of the National Socialism of Hitler. Pastor Trocmé always offered me the most complete and reliable assistance. No month went by when I did not turn to him for help; to him or to his friends or to the members of his congregation who were hiding Jews in that area. During all the tragic years of our resistance, Pastor Trocmé always answered our calls for help. He answered them with enthusiasm, even though he knew his efforts on our behalf endangered his life, those of his wife and children, and those of his congregation. His church and his home were among the great centres of the French resistance.

One night in February 1943, the Vichy police arrested Trocmé and two of his closest fellow conspirators, Pastor Édouard Theis and Roger Darcissac, a school principal. They spent more than a month in a prison camp, debating the rights and wrongs of violent resistance with hardheaded Communists and underground veterans. The first time they were offered their freedom, Trocmé and Theis refused to sign an oath of loyalty to Marshal Philippe Pétain's Vichy regime and all its works – on the grounds that, as men of God, once they had given their word, they would have had to keep it. A few days later, they were released regardless.

In 1971, André Trocmé became the first of the righteous of Le Chambon to be honoured by Israel. He had left the plateau after the war to promote the message of non-violence to a wider audience as European secretary of the Fellowship of Reconciliation; he then served as pastor of Saint-Gervais in Geneva. When the Israeli Consul-General in Paris, Yehuda Ben-David, telephoned to discuss arrangements for the award, Mme Trocmé told him that the pastor had had an operation and was slightly impeded by a stroke. The doctors promised a quick recovery. The ceremony was postponed, but soon afterwards Mme Trocmé informed Ben-David that her husband had died. His last wish was that he be cremated and his ashes buried in Le Chambon. On Saturday, 12 June 1971, a crowded congregation in the old, granite church where he had preached for a turbulent decade heard Theis read André Trocmé's last sermon, written fifteen hours before his death. His widow received the medal and certificate of the righteous among the nations from Ben-David on the pastor's behalf. Then she carried his ashes to the grave. His tombstone is inscribed: 'The peace of God passeth all understanding.'

· ● ·

In better times, young Albert Szajdholc felt, he might have enjoyed Christmas Eve in Andonno. The pitched roofs of the tiny Alpine village, about 6,000 feet above the Italian Riviera, were thick with snow. But in December 1943, all he and his family of Jewish refugees could think of, hiding from the German army in a two-storey outbuilding hugging a side wall of the Catholic church, was keeping warm. Albert, his parents and two younger sisters had little firewood and still less to eat. They sat wrapped in blankets, huddling as close to the hearth as possible. Their staple food was wild chestnuts, which grew in abundance on the mountainside. Sometimes they ate them raw, sometimes roasted, sometimes boiled for variety. Gradually, they had sold what few possessions they had kept in three years of running – his mother's gold earrings, gold from a broken denture – to supplement their diet. After trekking over the Alps from France three months earlier, the Szajdholcs had lived rough above Andonno, sleeping in shepherds' huts, or in the open. As winter set in, the village priest, Father Antonio Borsotto, offered them shelter in a sparsely furnished room beside the church, although the Germans were constantly searching Andonno and neighbouring villages for partisans and other fugitives. If they found any trace, they burned, looted and murdered. The priest, a stern, solemn-faced man in his early thirties, was aware of the risk he was taking. So were his flock. There were no secrets in Andonno. Another Jewish family – a woman, her son and daughter – was already being sheltered by a local teacher.

It was just before midnight on Christmas Eve. The church bells were echoing off the white mountain. From their window the Szajdholcs watched the peasant women, muffled in shawls, crunching through the snow on their way to mass. Forty years later, Albert still remembered the bitter cold and the dark sky alive with stars.

'We returned to the hearth and stared at the tiny flame as we reminisced about our own festive celebration of Hanukkah before the war. I closed my eyes and I could see my father lighting our beautiful silver *menorah* [candelabrum]. I could almost hear the sizzling of the traditional potato cakes being fried. . . . I shivered and returned to the not so pleasant present. We sat in a well of silence, each of us drawn into our dreams, when we heard someone rapping at the door. It was well past midnight and we looked at each other, a bit apprehensively. I opened the door a crack. Before me stood a wizened old woman, wrapped in a shawl. She handed me a package of cheese and then whispered a hoarse *"Buon Natale"*, a Merry Christmas. Stunned by her gift, we thanked her profusely. She seemed embarrassed by our gratitude and hurried away. Minutes later, there was another knock on the door. I opened it again, and this time a villager offered me a basket of firewood, wishing us *"Buon Natale"*. And then another woman came and brought us some bread. The villagers continued coming throughout the night, bringing us their gifts of food, clothing and wood. Poor people sharing with us from their own meagre resources. We were overcome. What had made them share with us, outsiders from a different country, believers in a different religion, strangers in their midst?'

The next morning broke bright and crisp. Christmas Day and the village was still and the world seemed at peace. Albert walked down the single, narrow street with its close-packed, flaking stucco houses. He met Giacomo Rosso, the local barber, wished him *'Buon Natale'* and then told him what had happened the night before. The barber put his hand on the nineteen-year-old Jew's shoulder and explained with a smile:

'In church last night, Father Borsotto told the story of the birth of our Saviour and the gifts brought to him by the Magi, as he does every Christmas. As usual he described how the Holy Family were lodged in a stable in Bethlehem, alone and friendless. And then how the Magi came with gifts for the Christ child. Father Borsotto then said, "Just as our Saviour couldn't find any lodging and was born in a manger, alone and rejected, so are Jews today alone and rejected. We have two Jewish families in our midst this Christmas and they too are alone, hungry, hunted for no reason except for being Jews.'' Father Borsotto then told us we could now be the Magi and bring gifts to the Jewish families in Andonno.'

Albert raced back to tell his parents. His father said, 'We are fortunate to be in Andonno, among good Christians.' He sent Albert to thank Father Borsotto. 'My son,' answered the priest, his eyes filling with tears, 'you don't have to thank me. It was the Christian thing to do.'

Although born in Warsaw, Albert had grown up in Brussels, where his father manufactured leather handbags. When the Germans invaded Belgium in 1940, the family fled with other Jews to southern France, hoping to escape to neutral Spain or Portugal. In Bayonne, the last town before the border, a hostile Polish consul refused to update their old passports. They were Jews, he said, not Poles. Without valid travel documents, they could not cross the Pyrenees. Instead, they took shelter in the village of St Martin Vesubie, above Nice, which was under Italian occupation. Benito Mussolini was Hitler's ally, but not his confederate in the extermination of European Jewry. He promulgated laws discriminating against Jews, but did not kill them.

When Mussolini signed an armistice with the Allies in September 1943, Albert and his family followed the Italian army back across the Alps to the spa of Valdieri. To their dismay, they found the Germans in control. Italy's war was not yet over. Along with other Jewish refugees, the Szajdholcs were ordered to assemble to be inspected for contraband. Few took this explanation at face value, but many complied, believing that they were bound for Paris. In fact, their destination was the Drancy deportation camp, en route to Auschwitz. Albert's father, Shlomo, was not deceived. He instructed his family to slip away and walk up the mountain. 'Don't stop, or turn around, not even if somebody calls to you,' he said. 'Stop only if you hear shooting.'

Chestnuts apart, the mountain was cold, wet and inhospitable. From time to time, the Jews heard shots from the road down below. Once Albert was almost caught by a German patrol. Albert's mother, Esther, discovered an unexpected talent for divining underground water sources. The fugitives preferred not to light a fire during the day for fear that somebody would see the smoke, but the villagers knew they were there. One day, Albert recounted, three strangers appeared from nowhere, a well-dressed man and woman, obviously city people, accompanied by a local farmer.

'We stared at the three and figured now we really had something to worry about. If they knew where we were and could so easily find us, anyone could. The man addressed us in Italian. We shook our heads, uncomprehending, and replied in French. Then, in a fairly good French, he told us that he had been visiting a nearby village, where one of the farmers reported that families with children were hiding in the mountains. He said he came up to satisfy his curiosity. We groaned. Now we knew it was no secret that we were up in the mountains.'

The refugees told the man that they were Jews running away from the Germans. He said that there was a Jewish community in the neighbouring town of Cuneo, where he lived, and agreed to take a letter to the local rabbi. In biblical Hebrew, they wrote that they needed money and shelter. Mrs Szajdholc gave the man her gold earrings to sell. He promised to return in a few days. When several days passed and he did not show up, they began to worry that he might have been an informer. But eventually he did return, with a letter, again written in biblical Hebrew, from the rabbi of Cuneo. The town's Jews, he wrote, were in a desperate plight. Most of them had disappeared, or were in hiding. It was impossible for him to help, but he hoped that God would be with them and protect them. Then the man handed Albert's mother the money for her earrings. 'We thanked this stranger', Albert wrote, 'and he left. We never knew who he was, nor did we ever see him again. We always felt there was something almost supernatural about the whole episode.'

The family began to buy extra food from Andonno, where they also picked up the latest news of the war. They made friends with the Rossis, a young married couple – he was Italian, she was French – who lived on the edge of the village. The Jews felt confident that the villagers would not betray them, but their new friends warned them to steer clear of Andonno's only Fascist.

'It was shortly after this warning,' Albert recalled, 'as we were coming into Andonno, that we spotted the Fascist sitting at the edge of the road. We stopped in our tracks, but there was no place to run. Besides, it was too late, he had seen us. He beckoned us over and spoke to us in halting French. "I know the villagers warned you to keep clear of me," he said. "It's true, I am a Fascist, but I have nothing against you people. You have no reason to be afraid of me. If I can help you in any way, I certainly will." ' He kept his word. Perhaps he could see how the tide was running. Perhaps, like other followers of Il Duce, he had no particular hostility towards Jews.

On another of Albert's visits, the Rossis persuaded him to stay for a party. There was nothing to worry about, they assured him. It would be just a few friends, one of whom turned out to be Father Borsotto.

'The party started in earnest,' Albert recorded. 'We roasted chestnuts and drank lots of wine. There was lots of reminiscing, then Father Borsotto, who had been a chaplain on the Russian front, described his experiences in Russia. The wine relaxed us, and soon Rossi turned to the priest and said, "Come on, show us how the Russians dance." Father Borsotto hesitated. Rossi turned to us and winked, putting his finger to his lips. "Remember, don't tell anyone what happened here tonight." Thus assured, the priest got up on the table, pulled up his cassock and began to do a kazatzka, a Cossak dance. We clapped and sang, encouraging him to continue his performance. I now knew that Father Borsotto was not as formidable as he looked.'

As autumn turned to winter, a freezing wind pierced the wooden slats of the Szajdholcs' mountain refuge. Snow was in the air, and they knew that they could not stay up there much longer. Albert's brother, Alter, nearly two years his senior, had already left with his young wife, Sidi, to find lodgings in Valdieri. Albert and his seventeen-year-old sister, Mariette, went down to Andonno to seek help from Father Borsotto. The priest began by reminding them that it was extremely dangerous to shelter soldiers, partisans or anyone else on the run from the Wehrmacht. 'The Germans have warned us that if they find partisans or even abandoned army uniforms in a village, they will burn down the house and maybe even worse,' he frowned. They were not bluffing. A week after Christmas, a German truck filled with soldiers was attacked by partisans in Boves, a nearby village. They killed several soldiers before retreating into the mountains. The Germans retaliated by destroying the entire village. The priest was burned alive in his locked church.

In Andonno, Father Borsotto shook his head and paused for a moment, then told Albert and Mariette, 'I know it's impossible for you to stay in the mountains through the winter. I will try to help you.' That was how the Szajdholc family came to be in the room beside the church on Christmas Eve. Father Borsotto handed Albert the key and advised them to move in at night. 'The villagers, of course, will know that you are in the room,' he added. 'That doesn't concern me. I am only concerned about strangers who might come by. Please tell your family to be very cautious.'

The winter of 1943 was hard for everyone, not just the refugees. One day Albert saw men digging a pit in a neighbour's back yard. 'Listen, young man,' one of them warned him, 'what you see here you keep to yourself. You understand? We are burying food and seeds to avoid starvation.' The Germans and the partisans, he explained, were living off the land. They came and took everything the peasants had. 'If they take all our food, we shall have nothing to eat for the next two years. So we have no choice but to hide some seeds for the next crop.'

By now Albert had picked up a smattering of Italian. He heard that a school-teacher, Caterina Destefanis, was sheltering a French Jewess, Regina Gal, and her two small children. Mme Gal's husband had been deported from Paris. The families became friends. Albert also befriended Giacomo Rosso, who doubled as the village barber and the village tailor. While in France, Albert had obtained false papers in the name of Raymond Bermond. In Italy the villagers called him Raimondo.

Albert would drop into Giacomo's shop to catch up with the news. Giacomo had a strong, craggy face and a head of thick, black hair. He limped from a childhood illness. They were chatting amiably when out of the blue Giacomo suggested that the young Jew should become a barber. He needed an assistant so that he could have more time for tailoring. Albert protested: 'What do I know about being a barber? I've never shaved anyone.' Giacomo would not take 'No' for an answer. 'It's easy, Raimondo. Don't you shave yourself?' So, Albert/Raimondo became the barber's reluctant apprentice. His first customer proved a disaster:

'I soaped him up and worked the lather well and then turned to

Giacomo, expecting him to take over. Giacomo thrust his chin out and nodded his head, indicating that I was to proceed. I took the razor and began stropping it as I had seen the barber do so many times before. Somehow the heavily lathered man had a feeling something wasn't right. My hand trembled as I began shaving him. I cleared the neck all right, then made my way to his upper lip, holding the razor at too sharp an angle. And then it happened. I nicked his nostril and the man shrieked. Giacomo came running with a styptic pencil, but to my horror the blood continued flowing. Thank God the bleeding finally stopped. Giacomo then turned to me and said, "Finish the job." The man screeched, "Oh no!" That was the end of my barbering career.'

The refugees' idyllic Christmas proved to be no more than an interlude. Andonno was off the main road, but the Germans were coming too often for comfort. The Szajdholcs heard on the grapevine that Hungary, an ally of Hitler's, was issuing travel documents to Jews. Albert's sister-in-law, Sidi, volunteered to go to Rome with her mother and see the Hungarian consul. Their family came from Czechoslovakia, formerly part of the Austro-Hungarian Empire, and spoke Hungarian. While they were away, Albert's brother Alter rejoined the Szajdholcs in Andonno. A few days later, Mariette was sent to the nearest town with a neighbour's daughter, Marianna Giordano, to buy suitcases. They were preparing to move on, but soon after Mariette had left the family heard the clatter of gunfire in the mountains. A very agitated Father Borsotto pounded on their door. 'You must leave the village immediately,' he urged. 'The Germans are attacking the partisans. If they find you here, they'll burn down the village.' The Jewish family grabbed their coats and struggled up a steep path behind the house. Albert ran back to warn Mme Gal and her children.

'When I reached her place, I was told she had already left, so I ran back to our house. Alter was waiting for me and we both made our way up as quickly as we could. We could hear shots just behind us. As we reached a bend in the track, bullets ricocheted off the rocks. At last we rejoined the rest of the family. We were not alone. Many of the young men from the village had also made their way to the mountain top. They had heard that the Germans were hunting for young Italians to force them into the army.

'There was a tiny shed, and Alter and I decided to check it out and see if it could serve as a shelter. We were close to the shed when a direct hit blew it to bits. The shepherds' huts had become prime targets for German artillery and bombing. The Germans knew that partisans used these huts, and they were determined to destroy them. We looked up and saw 'planes heading towards us. We dived into the snow and tried to camouflage ourselves. We could see houses in Boves and Tettobandito burning. At long last the firing stopped and the young men headed back to Andonno, but we couldn't join them. We had no place to go.'

Luckily, the Jewish family found a hut that had somehow been overlooked by the bombers. Despite the risk of another raid, they had no choice but to take shelter there. It was icy cold, but they did not dare light a fire for fear of drawing attention to themselves. All they could do was sit huddled together shivering. Towards evening they saw Mariette hurrying up the mountain. She and Marianna had heard the shooting, but had stayed in town until it was over. Marianna's parents, Usebio and Anna Giordano, were worried about the Szajdholc family. They knew it was impossible to stay overnight in the mountains without shelter, so they had sent Mariette to tell them to come back after nightfall. They would leave their barn door unlocked, but the Jews would have to return to the mountains by daybreak.

The first thing Albert did was to go back to the room beside the church to pick up some of their belongings. It was only then that he discovered how close a call it had been. German soldiers had ransacked the room. Clothes were scattered everywhere. Albert's father had left behind his *tefillin*, the leather straps and boxes which observant Jews bind on their arms and foreheads every day during morning prayers. Evidently, the Germans had not known what they were. If they had realized that Jews had been hiding there, they would surely have burned the house and the church, and perhaps even executed Father Borsotto.

The Giordanos kept a grocery store in the village. They had two daughters, Marianna and Anna, who had often played with the Jewish girls. Like everyone else in Andonno, they now knew how ruthless the Germans could be. Many of their neighbours in Boves had been killed during the search operation. The village had been surrounded and anyone trying to escape had been shot. Yet regardless of the danger, the Giordanos left the barn door open every night.

'In the winter in these mountain villages, it wasn't unusual for people to sleep in barns [Albert remembered]. They were often warmer than the houses. The first night in the barn Signora Giordano greeted us and instructed us to hang our shoes from the rafters. If not, the rabbits would gnaw them to pieces. The rabbits also came into the barn to keep warm.

'Every night, when we came in from the freezing cold, a pot of soup awaited us. Thanks to their compassion and generosity, we slept in the straw, warmed by the body heat of the animals. In the mornings, Signora Giordano prepared fresh straw for us. One day, while we were shivering in the snow up above, we were startled to see an old woman, swathed in black, making her way laboriously up the mountain. She was carrying a pot of hot soup for us. We could never find the words to thank these good simple people.'

By the spring of 1944, Andonno's conspiracy of goodness came to an end. Sidi returned from Rome with Hungarian papers for the entire family. She had managed to convince the consul that the Polish-Belgian Szajdholcs were Hungarians. Albert became Alex Vamos from Budapest. The family went by train to Florence, then to Rome, where they stayed until the liberation. After the war, they settled in New York.

In 1984, Albert, by then living in Jerusalem, having changed his surname from the Polish Szajdholc to the Hebrew Sharon, went back to Andonno with his wife Lynn. In the village square, they saw a woman washing clothes in a well. She told them that she was too young to remember the war, but she knew a woman who had helped Jews. It was Caterina Destefanis, the school-teacher who had sheltered Mme Gal and her children. Albert was able to tell her that they, too, had reached New York. Signora Destefanis, now in her seventies, took them to the pastel-pink and blue house beside the church. Suddenly, the Sharons were surrounded by village women. Albert asked if anyone knew Giacomo the barber. One of the women said that she was his wife, but that he was now very sick and could not see anyone. Albert persuaded her to take him to her house. The old man came down. He peered at Albert, but said that he had never seen him before. Albert started to remind him that he had once been his assistant. Suddenly, the frail barber smiled, tapped his nostril, raised an eyebrow and roared, 'Raimondo!'

2

The Honourable Consuls

If Giorgio Perlasca had not been a Fascist, he would not have been in a position to rescue between 3,000 and 6,000 Hungarian Jews from deportation and death, and he would not have won a place in the honourable company of consuls and attachés, diplomats and semi-diplomats – a Swede, a Japanese, a German, a Portuguese and two International Red Cross men – who gambled their careers, sometimes their lives, to deny Hitler his Final Solution. Perlasca was a Fascist in the Italian style, not a Nazi, not an anti-Semite. Born in Como in 1910 and raised in Padua, he was the son of an unadventurous family of Catholic functionaries. His grandfather had been a senior official in the service of the Italian royal house. His father was a town clerk. Giorgio was a dedicated supporter of Mussolini. After studying in a technical high school, he served in the Italian army – as a conscript in the conquest of Abyssinia and as a volunteer on Franco's side in the Spanish Civil War, where he rose to the rank of lieutenant in the artillery. He fought at Guernica, which, he insisted, 'was not as badly destroyed as Picasso made out'. The Spanish connection saved his liberty, if not his life, in Budapest in the dog days of Hitler's war. It certainly saved the lives of his Jewish protégés. He remained loyal to Mussolini, with dwindling enthusiasm, until Il Duce's downfall with the armistice of September 1943. 'Before the armistice,' he told me in Jerusalem forty-six years later, 'I had supported Mussolini, but I was against the war and against the axis with Germany. When he entered the war, and especially after the armistice, I didn't feel I was a Fascist any more. I was not anti-Fascist, but I was anti-Nazi.'

Perlasca avoided mobilization in 1939 because he was living abroad, though he was ready to rejoin the army if he had been called. Instead, he spent the first four years of the war as the Budapest representative of an import-export firm buying tinned meat for the Italian navy. His beat also included Sofia, Belgrade and Bucharest. When Mussolini fell, Perlasca decided not to go back to Italy. As a known adherent of the discredited regime, he was unsure of his reception. At the same time, his status in pro- Nazi Hungary had deteriorated. He was no longer a friendly alien. In the spring and summer of 1944, the Hungarian authorities interned him with the consul-general and other Italians in a village outside the capital. Perlasca got away on 13 October 1944. 'I escaped almost legally,' he smiled. 'Sweden was protecting Italian citizens. A Swedish delegation came to check our conditions. I had temporary permission to go with the delegation to Budapest. I never came back.'

Two days later, the Hungarian Arrow Cross Fascists seized power and Budapest collapsed into chaos. Perlasca felt more vulnerable than ever. He feared that the new Government, or its German allies, would throw him into prison. It was at this point that he remembered a promise by General Francisco Franco to protect anyone who had fought with the Falangists in Spain. He went to the Spanish Legation and asked for citizenship, which was granted on the spot. The Hungarian Interior Ministry had no qualms about registering him as a Spanish citizen. Spain was neutral, but friendly.

Perlasca had lived in Budapest long enough to understand what was happening in the city. He could see that anti-Semitism was getting worse, and he knew that the Spanish Legation, along with other diplomatic missions, was trying to help Jews. Franco was an ally of Hitler's, but had kept Spain out of the war and was careful to distance himself from the Nazis' extermination campaign against European Jewry. In the late nineteenth century, Spain had been swept by a wave of remorse for the expulsion of its own Jews in 1492. Jews in the Ottoman Empire who could prove their Spanish descent were offered their citizenship back. Spain was the first nation to give Russian Jews a haven from the Czarist pogroms. In the same spirit, Franco provided Spanish protection to Sephardi Jews under Nazi occupation (especially in the last years of the war, when it was clear that Germany was losing). Within twenty-four hours of becoming an honorary Spaniard, Perlasca volunteered his services. The head of mission, Angel Sanz-Briz, who had already sent dozens of Jews to Switzerland, issued the Italian businessman with a card identifying him as a Spanish consular official.

'I was never pushed to take the initiative,' he recalled. 'The Hungarian Jews didn't know me, but I saw the situation and I felt that something had to be done. I couldn't ignore it. It was dangerous, but everything was dangerous at that time. I saw people outside the legation, fighting and pleading. I asked who they were. The diplomat said they were Sephardi Jews seeking Spanish protection. There were only five or six Sephardi families in Budapest. The rest were Ashkenazi, but we pretended they were Sephardi so that we could protect them.'

Perlasca's relations with Jews before the war had been warm, but limited. 'My family were church-going Catholics,' he said, 'but we were educated to respect other people. I always thought that Catholics, Protestants and Jews were the same. I met Jews at school and outside. In Padua we were close to the Bassani family and the Serravalle families. I also became friendly with a Jew from Fiume whom I met in Abyssinia.'

When he began working with the Spanish Legation, there were about 300 Jews under its protection. Towards the end of November, with the Soviet army closing in on Budapest, some neutral governments instructed their ambassadors to leave. By then, according to Perlasca, the Spaniards were sheltering about 3,000 Jews in eight safe-houses. On 30 November 1944, Perlasca woke to find that Sanz-Briz had gone, leaving no replacement. The Italian assumed that he expected him to continue looking after the Jews, though he left him a note saying that he could obtain a visa to Switzerland through the Spanish Embassy in Vienna. He chose to stay, bravely and inventively defending 'his' Jews. He went on issuing protective passes, sealed with Sanz-Briz's stamp and all pre-dated to early November. At any point the authorities might have challenged his credentials and found them suicidally flimsy.

'There was no official letter appointing me chargé d'affaires, but the Foreign Ministry in Madrid later backed me up. At first, I didn't know what to do, but then I began to feel like a fish in water. I continued giving out passes and looked after the Jews in the safe-houses flying the Spanish flag. As the proverb says, opportunity makes the thief.

'The Hungarian Nazis started coming into the safe-houses to take the Jews away. I went to them and said, "You must leave these people alone. I am here, here is the flag." I was the only official left and the only Christian. The Hungarians took them out, but I managed to get them back. The Hungarians were anxious that Spain should not close the legation. They believed it would provide an open line to the Allies as the war came to an end. I said, "You want us to stay, you give us more Jews." I gave the authorities documents saying these Jews were Sephardim and were under our protection. I kept doing this until the Russians arrived.'

It looked as if his bluff was being called in the second week of January 1945, when the Hungarian Interior Minister, Gabor Vajna, decreed that all the Jews in foreign missions should be taken to one place and killed. But Perlasca was not finished:

'I went to see Vajna at the Ministry. I sat with him for two and a half hours, trying to persuade him to let the Jews stay. At first Vajna insisted that the Jews had to be wiped out. I said, "If you don't assure us the Jews can stay in our houses, the Spanish Government will arrest 3,000 Hungarians in Spain and it will persuade Brazil and Uruguay to do the same in their countries." I made this up. I went on, "Hungarian people will soon pay for whatever you do to the Jews. If you want to protect your people, you must protect the Jews. Otherwise, your people will pay the price." Vajna said, "You're blackmailing me. We have to destroy the Jews." I said, "The situation will be very tragic for both peoples." Budapest was already under siege by the Russians. Vajna started to cry. He replied, "The Jews in your hands can stay. The status quo will be honoured." I tried to persuade him to honour the status quo for Jews protected by other missions, but he refused.'

The next day a Hungarian official asked for proof that the threat of retaliation was indeed government policy. Perlasca had no such proof, but immediately sent a telegram to Madrid. 'I didn't know if anyone would understand what I was talking about, but after two days a telegram came back saying they were very pleased that I had reached the status quo agreement with Vajna.'

One of the Jews who owed his life to Perlasca was Avraham Ronai, a twelve-year-old messenger boy for the Budapest Jewish community, who was to become a leading actor with the Habimah theatre in Tel Aviv. Avraham found shelter in one of the Spanish safe-houses with his mother and sister. They lived seven to ten people to a room. Perlasca, he testified, came to the house almost every day, bringing powdered milk and food. One day a squad of Arrow Cross men broke into the house, lined up all the adults and prepared to march them to the Danube and shoot them. Avraham was spared because of his age, but his mother and sister were taken. Suddenly Perlasca walked into the hallway and demanded, 'Who is in charge here?' Avraham, who was watching the drama from a spiral staircase, saw him walk up to an officer and shout in bad German, 'How dare you behave like this on the property of a friendly country? I insist that you release these people, otherwise you will be in trouble with your superiors. If I have to cable Madrid about this violation of Spanish interests, there will be grave consequences.' The officer apologized and ordered his men to set the Jews free.

Most of Perlasca's trials of strength were with the Hungarian Fascists, but he had some brushes with the Germans. One day he went with a Swedish colleague, Raoul Wallenberg, to the railway station. They were trying to rescue Jews from being transported to Auschwitz. Perlasca picked out a boy and a girl aged about twelve. An SS major threatened him with a pistol and pushed the children back in line. Wallenberg told the SS man, 'This is my colleague.' The major retorted, 'He is disturbing my work.' Wallenberg snapped back, 'You call this work?' At that point an SS colonel intervened. 'Leave the youngsters,' he ordered. 'Their turn will come.' When Perlasca asked Wallenberg who the colonel was, he said that he was Adolf Eichmann, the man entrusted by Hitler to make sure the trains ran on time and the Jews reached the gas chambers. Fifteen years later, when Israeli agents abducted Eichmann from his Argentinian retreat and brought him to trial in Jerusalem, two Germans asked Perlasca to testify for the defence. He refused.

Wallenberg was the inspiration for rescue efforts by other neutral envoys in Budapest. Sweden was the first country to embrace a 1944 American initiative to aid and rescue Jews.

Wallenberg set himself a single mission: to stop as many as possible from being deported, using Swedish passports and funds donated by American Jewish charities. Historians estimate that the consuls' campaign may have saved as many as 100,000 Hungarian Jews, though a majority of these owed their salvation to copies of the consuls' documents forged by Zionist youth groups. At a minimum estimate, Giorgio Perlasca was responsible for saving 3,000 of these. The Hungarians put the figure at 5,200. Perlasca argued that this was the number directly protected by Spain. 'I also managed to protect some outside the official houses,' he said. 'The overall total is more like 6,000.' Although he was in touch with the other envoys, he found that by the time he was operating they had forfeited any influence they might have had. 'The Hungarians hated the Swedes and the others,' he explained. 'To achieve anything I had to act alone.'

His last encounter with Wallenberg took place as he was leaving the Interior Ministry after the confrontation with Gabor Vajna. Fearing that his luck was running out, the Swedish diplomat asked to be taken into the Spanish legation. 'I offered to take Wallenberg to the Legation in my car, which had a Spanish flag and a police escort. He said he couldn't come straight away. He had something to see to. He would come in the afternoon and bring his car. He never came, and I never saw him again.'

When the Red Army marched into Budapest, Perlasca destroyed his Spanish passport and diplomatic papers. 'I burned the Spanish flag and all the documents and became Italian again. I was protected by the Swedes.' Franco had served his purpose. It was no longer convenient to work for a Fascist regime. Perlasca soon made his way back to Italy, where he was active for a while in the campaign to keep Trieste Italian. Then he returned to his family in Padua.

In Jerusalem in 1989, Israel honoured him as one of the righteous among the nations. At seventy-nine he was a tall, gaunt figure with thick-rimmed glasses, grey crew cut and an air of hopes unfulfilled. He might have been taken for a retired middle-grade civil servant, or a retired schoolmaster. When I asked what he had done since the war, he replied, 'I had lost everything in Hungary. I couldn't settle down to business. Italy was different. All my ideals had come to nothing. Somehow I managed.' Pressed to be more specific, he smiled, 'No comment.' They were the first words he had spoken in English. Then he added in Italian, 'I did everything but steal.'

• ● •

Sempo Sugihara, the Japanese Consul in Kovno (now Kaunas), was not what he seemed. His Government had sent Sugihara, a Russian-language teacher, to the Lithuanian capital at the end of 1939 because, with the signing of the Molotov–Ribbentrop Pact, Tokyo was anxious to monitor Soviet–German relations. Lithuania was enjoying a precarious freedom between Hitler's hammer and Stalin's anvil. The Japanese were looking ahead to their own pact with Germany and Italy. In plain words, Sugihara was a spy. Until 23 July 1940, he issued not a single visa. That was not what he was there for. However, over the next month, he signed hundreds a day – all for Jews fleeing Poland before the Nazi invader. The recipients included Dr Zorach Warhaftig, a future Israeli Religious Affairs Minister, and Menahem Savidor, a future Speaker of the Knesset, Israel's parliament, as well as all the 300 staff and students of the celebrated Mir *yeshivah*. Mir, founded in 1815, was the only one of Europe's twenty major *yeshivot* to survive the war intact. By the end of each working day Sugihara's hands were so stiff that his wife, Sachiko, had to massage them back to life. Three times his Government ordered him to stop, three times he defied instructions. During a visit to Israel three decades later, he told Warhaftig, 'I saw your plight, and I thought I should help.' Even though it cost him dearly after the war, he had no regrets.

The story which earned the forty-year-old Japanese spy an unlikely chapter in the annals of Jewish rescue began when two Dutch seminarists, who had been studying at the Polish Telz *yeshivah*, approached the Dutch Consul in the hope of finding asylum in one of the colonies. The Consul, Jan Zwartendijk, told them that the only possible destinations were Curaçao and Surinam in the Caribbean. He agreed to write in their passports that entry was permitted without visas. With the blessing of his superior, the Netherlands ambassador in Riga, he left out the standard qualification: 'Subject to the consent of the governor.' The students, Nathan Gutwirth and Leo Sternheim, knew that once they had what could pass for an entry permit to a final destination, other consuls might grant them transit visas to get out of Europe.

Gutwirth and Sternheim reported to Warhaftig, then a thirty-three-year-old lawyer and leader of the Hehalutz Hamizrahi (religious pioneers) movement, who had set up a committee in Kovno to help Jewish refugees emigrate to Palestine. Warhaftig sent the students back to ask Zwartendijk whether he would issue similar endorsements to Polish Jews. The Consul agreed. Immediately, the Dutch consulate was besieged. 'The consulate staff applied themselves diligently,' Warhaftig testified, 'and not a single applicant was turned away.' The Dutch claimed to have issued 1,200–1,400 permits. Many more were forged and copied. Warhaftig confessed that they were a bluff. 'There was never any intention of going to Curaçao,' he told me fifty years after the event, 'and none of the Polish Jews tried it.' It was, perhaps, as well. In the 1970s, Warhaftig happened to meet the man who had been governor of Curaçao at the time. He had been posted as ambassador to Jerusalem. When Warhaftig asked him what he would have done if hundreds of Jewish refugees had turned up, he replied, 'I would have sent them back on the high seas.'

None the less, the Dutch permits offered a key to escape. Sempo Sugihara held the lock. Warhaftig sounded him out. They conversed in broken English. The Jewish leader recalled:

'He knew we couldn't go back to Poland. We were not Lithuanian citizens, we were not Russian citizens. So we had to flee. He had some sympathy for us. People came with visas for Curaçao. The only way was via Japan. So why not? No damage would be done to Japan if they stayed for a few weeks. He was a liberal-minded person who looked askance at Nazi Germany. Gradually, he felt he was doing something special.

'The consulate was a very modest one, a few rooms. Long queues of Jews formed in the street. They were quiet queues. There had been a great discussion about whether it was worth getting the visas or not, but we knew there was only a short time. It was known that all the consulates would be liquidated. Once the Russians took over, there would be no place for consulates or embassies there. In the last days the queues were very long.'

In retrospect, Sugihara was amazed at his own courage. He told a Japanese interviewer: 'Someone had to make a sacrifice to save all those lives. I looked at all those people clinging to the iron fences of the consulate begging for visas, and I thought I just had to do something for them. In pure joy, they would fall to their knees in thanks. I was so inspired by the sight that I worked non-stop for a month writing visas.'

Queues outside the consulate were so long that applicants had to wait for three days. The Consul had no illusions about the Curaçao 'visas'. During his 1969 visit to Israel, he explained that he had been well aware of their fictitious character, but so long as he was doing nothing illegal, he had been prepared to help. By his own count, Sugihara saved 4,500 Jews. Alex Triguboff, a member of Japan's small Jewish business community who volunteered to help them clear immigration control, put the number as high as 10,000. 'Sometimes they'd just photographed one person's visa,' he confided to a correspondent of the London *Times* in 1985. 'Again and again I saw the same name and the same date on the visa.' Warhaftig dismissed all these estimates as exaggerations. His tally, based on his own records, was 2,500. No one disputes that Sugihara worked till he dropped, or that he put his career in jeopardy. He and his wife were still signing papers as the train pulled out of the Soviet-occupied Kovno station after he had been ordered to close the consulate at the end of August 1940. A year later, in June 1941, the Germans drove the Russians out of Kovno. They and their Lithuanian collaborators slaughtered thousands of Jews before the Red Army recaptured the city in 1944.

From Lithuania, Sugihara went on to serve as Japanese Consul-General in Nazi-occupied Prague and Bucharest. At the end of the war, he and his family were interned for a year and a half by the Russians. When he finally arrived back in Tokyo, he submitted his resignation to the Foreign Ministry, a formality required of all who had served the defeated wartime regime. Most returning diplomats received an official recommendation for work in the private sector, but Sugihara was denied such assistance. He was told that this was because he had defied orders in helping the Jews in Kovno. At first he earned his living as a door-to-door salesman, then managed a United States army PX store near Tokyo before serving for sixteen years as Moscow representative of the Kawakami trading company.

Sugihara was invited to Israel in 1969, when his son was awarded a scholarship to study at the Hebrew University of Jerusalem. By the time he was honoured by Yad Vashem in 1985, he was too frail to attend the award ceremony at the Israeli Embassy in Tokyo. He died a year later aged eighty-six. The Mir *yeshivah*, relocated in Brooklyn, established a Sempo Sugihara scholarship fund to commemorate the fiftieth anniversary of the Kovno rescue and invited his son, Hiroki, to a festive dinner in a New York hotel. 'It is fifty years after the rescue,' the *yeshivah* president, Rabbi Moses Kalmanowitz, told the *Jerusalem Post*, 'and it reminded us we never gave our thanks.'

The Kovno Jews, armed with their Curaçao declarations and Japanese transit visas, made their way by train to Moscow, then by the Trans-Siberian Railway to Vladivostok, a journey of about ten days. 'My wife and few-months-old son came with me,' Warhaftig remembered. 'We travelled in organized groups. We took food with us. The smallest groups were about ten people, the largest several hundred. From Vladivostok we went by boat to Kobe, and from there overland to Tokyo and Yokohama, where I established my headquarters. From there I organized emigration of the refugees, to Israel and to Shanghai.'

The refugees were helped by the Jewish business community of Kobe – and by a Japanese professor, who deserves a footnote to this story, if not the honour of one of the righteous among the nations. Setsuzo Kotzuji was descended from a long line of Shinto priests. As a young man, he began a private search for a different god. He studied the Bible, which led him to Christianity, but that too failed to satisfy his quest. The arrival of the pious Jews, with their black hats and beards, whetted his appetite. He had already published a grammar of the Hebrew language in Japanese and was eager to learn more about Jewish faith and customs. Having read an interview with Warhaftig in a Japanese newspaper, he presented himself at the future Cabinet Minister's door. They talked in Hebrew and English.

'My own command of English at the time was rather limited,' Warhaftig admitted, 'and Kotzuji's Hebrew was biblical and halting, although he knew several Psalms by heart. Our talks therefore proceeded at a slow pace and were interrupted by long silences that gave us time for reflection. There was a distinct ceremonial element to the procedure.

'He served as our interpreter. When I visited the Foreign Ministry or the police, he came with me. He was our friend in a foreign country. He was respected by the authorities. One of a small group he ran for the study of Judaism was a relative of the Mikado.'

Kotzuji also claimed to have helped some of the Kovno Jews to extend their Japanese visas. In 1959, he went to Israel and asked to be converted to Judaism. At first Warhaftig was not enthusiastic, but, when Kotzuji convinced him that he was in earnest, he agreed to help. His old mentor served as *sandak* (godfather) when the Japanese scholar was ritually circumcized at Sha'are Zedek hospital in Jerusalem.

Fourteen years later, Michael Shilo, a young diplomat at the Israeli embassy in Tokyo, received a telephone call from Marvin Tokayer, the American rabbi of the city's Jewish community. Professor Kotzuji, he reported, was dying of cancer in Yokohama. Shilo had never heard of him, but was persuaded that he had once helped Jews and deserved a visit. They decided to go and see him the following week, but a couple of days before their intended trip the rabbi telephoned again to say that it was too late. Kotzuji had died, but in his will he had asked to be buried in Jerusalem. Could the Embassy help? Shilo had his doubts:

'This was October 1973, just three days after the beginning of the Yom Kippur War. I said it was very unlikely that anyone in Israel would have the time or the patience for such a story when the Syrians were almost in Tiberias. The rabbi said one of the people Kotzuji had helped was now the Minister of Religious Affairs, Zorach Warhaftig. Maybe he could help. "Please cable him and tell him." Very reluctantly I did so: "Professor Kotzuji of Yokohama, whom you may remember, has died and asked to be buried in Jerusalem." I got a telex back saying: "Do everything that's necessary and send him." The body arrived in Jerusalem in the middle of the war. Hundreds of Hassidim marched to the cemetery, where he was given a Jewish burial.'

• • •

On 19 September 1943, Georg Ferdinand Duckwitz, the German Shipping Attaché in Copenhagen, wrote in his diary: 'I know what I have to do.' What this loyal servant of the Third Reich, the confidant of Hitler's plenipotentiary, Werner Best, had to do was to thwart plans to deport Denmark's 7,700 Jews to the concentration camps. He did so with such persistence and conviction that all but 472 of the Jews escaped one jump ahead of the Gestapo. Between 26 September and 12 October, in one of the epic, spontaneous rescues of the war, about 6,000 full Jews and 1,300 part Jews were smuggled by fishing boat across the sound to neutral Sweden. It was a victory for the people of Denmark, who had resisted all discrimination against the Jewish minority and were ready to risk their lives for them, but without Duckwitz's early warning they would not have been able to mobilize in time. What the Attaché had heard from his chief on 19 September was that a small fleet of German transport vessels would anchor in Copenhagen harbour ten days later to ferry the entire Jewish population to the camps. A special SS unit had already arrived. Adolf Eichmann's deputy, Rolf Günther, was in the capital to supervise the 'lightning raid'.

Jorgen Haestrup, a leading Danish historian of the Nazi occupation, wrote: 'His warning staved off full disaster.' Leni Yahil, an Israeli researcher, added, 'Duckwitz's efforts were unique, and we know about no other high-ranking German official who fulfilled such an important role in the rescue of the Jews, certainly putting his own life in great danger.' Hans Hedtoft, a future Prime Minister and one of the Social Democratic leaders to whom Duckwitz leaked the deportation plan, commented in 1946, 'He was one of those men who made one put one's faith in a new Germany.'

Duckwitz had lived in Denmark since 1928. After graduating from law school, he was posted to Copenhagen as the agent of a German coffee merchant. He spoke Danish and had many friends in the local business and political communities. After the German invasion in April 1940, he was recruited as Shipping Attaché. Like many young Germans, he had been attracted to the Nazi Party, but by the early 1940s he had drifted away. According to Haestrup, 'He had turned against the whole political line of the Party, its terror and violence in Germany and the occupied countries. In particular, Duckwitz was full of disgust at the inhuman treatment of the Jews by the Nazis.'

The occupation of Denmark was unique. Until the summer of 1943, the Germans allowed King Christian x to remain on his throne. A more-or-less independent government, with its own armed forces, police and civil service, continued to function – with the acquiescence of the people. Unlike neighbouring Norway, this was not a Quisling regime. It collaborated, but on its own terms as well as the Germans'. The Jews remained not only free, but protected. Historians have debunked the popular legend that the King threatened that he and his family would be the first to don the yellow star if Jews were forced to wear it. Nor, it seems, did he attend a synagogue service after the Germans had proposed to introduce anti-Jewish legislation. But most historians agree that, even though the legends were not true, they might as well have been. 'It is clear to all', a Swedish observer noted, 'that the King watches over Denmark's dignity, that he shows where to draw the line.' One of the places where Christian x drew the line was the equality of his Jewish subjects. In December 1941, after Danish Nazis set fire to a synagogue, the King publicly regretted the act. Later he wrote to Duckwitz's boss, Werner Best: 'I desire to stress to you – not only because of human concern for the citizens of my country, but also because of fear of further consequences in future relations between Germany and Denmark – that special measures in regard to a group of people who have enjoyed full rights of citizenship for more than one hundred years would have the most severe consequences.'

Sympathy for 'our Jewish fellow-citizens' was so widespread that even the Germans had to take it into account. Danish Nazi groups were a discredited minority. The synagogue arsonists were arrested by the Danish police, tried and sent to prison for three years and twenty days. The editor of an anti-Semitic magazine was sentenced to 100 days for libelling a department store owner who employed a Jewish secretary. When the editor appealed, the court increased the sentence to 160 days.

Best and his superiors tolerated this Nordic eccentricity because Germany needed Danish goodwill. Throughout the war, Denmark was a major food supplier to the Reich. In 1942, some 3.6 million Germans received their meat, pork and butter rations from Denmark. A year later it rose to 4.6 million, and by 1944 had soared to 8.4 million. Continuation of that supply was a German priority. If the price was suspension of the Final Solution of the Jewish problem, Germany was willing to pay. The alternative, the plenipotentiary and his colleagues were convinced, would have provoked large-scale social and economic disruption. The Danish people, as the King's letter hinted, would have ceased to co-operate.

Best, who was posted to Copenhagen in 1942, was a Nazi by career and by conviction. He would have had no moral inhibition about deporting or persecuting the Jews, but his brief was to keep Denmark quiet. In the spring and summer of 1943, circumstances conspired to change his stand. Elections in March gave the Government of Erik Scavenius a resounding vote of confidence. The Danish Nazis were routed. The result was celebrated, by the Prime Minister and the voters, as an assertion of Danish independence. But what the politicians had not calculated on was an escalation of active resistance throughout the country – sabotage supported by political strikes – all reinforced by a growing impression that the tide of war was finally turning against the Germans. The Danes were speeding the conqueror on his way. At the same time, Best was engaged in a power struggle with his military opposite number, Lieutenant-General Hermann von Hanneken. Hitler was losing patience. A German officer had been severely beaten by rioters. On 29 August, the Reich imposed a state of emergency and Hanneken took control. The Government resigned, parliament dissolved itself and King Christian declared himself a prisoner of war. The Danish navy scuttled twenty-nine of its warships; thirteen others escaped into Swedish waters.

On 8 September, Best sent a telegram to Berlin recommending that 'measures should now be taken towards a solution of the problems of the Jews and the freemasons'. In order to arrest and deport the Jews 'at one sweep', he requested the dispatch of security police. Best seems to have been less concerned about the Jews than about grappling back control from the military. Once he had the police at his disposal, he could use them to quell the resistance and restore his power base. The army, which, as he pointed out, knew nothing of Danish affairs, could return to barracks. In the short term, this ploy worked. The security police were duly dispatched. Best, seen to be taking a strong Nazi initiative, was reinstated.

Whether he intended to follow through with the deportations can never be known, but Berlin took him at his word and authorized him to go ahead. On 11 September, he briefed Duckwitz, who was furious and threatened to resign. Duckwitz told Best that he would be ashamed to remain a member of his staff if Best persecuted the Jews. Best replied that, while he shared Duckwitz's distaste, they had to obey orders. The Shipping Attaché claimed later that this altercation persuaded his chief to think again – and to send him to Berlin to explain why the time was not right for action against the Jews. This first mission failed. Duckwitz's 'plane arrived too late. Hitler had approved the operation and instructed the SS chief, Heinrich Himmler, to solve all the technical problems. Back in Copenhagen, Best showed Duckwitz Berlin's response. It was then that the troubled Attaché confided to his diary that he knew what he had to do.

He turned next to Stockholm, where he pretended to have official business. With the help of a Swedish diplomat, a secret meeting was arranged at the home of the Prime Minister, Per Albin Hansson. Duckwitz informed Hansson of the danger facing Danish Jews and urged him to offer them a haven in Sweden. After consulting his Cabinet, the Prime Minister agreed to receive the Jewish refugees, provided that Germany agreed. Predictably, Berlin ignored Stockholm's overture. Once again, Duckwitz had tried and failed. At most, he had ensured that the Swedes were not totally surprised when the fishing boats started arriving on their side of the sound.

Three days later, on 28 September, the final order to carry out the deportation reached Copenhagen. Best reported back that the order would be implemented 'during this week – probably between 1 and 2 October'. Again, he kept Duckwitz posted. Again, the Attaché did what he had to do. That Tuesday afternoon, he sought a meeting with his contacts in the Social Democratic Party. When he walked into their headquarters, Hans Hedtoft remembered, he was 'white with indignation and shame'. In a few anguished sentences, he told the Danish politicians that the Jews were doomed. Within seventy-two hours, German ships would berth in Copenhagen harbour and the Jews would be rounded up and transported to their fate. Duckwitz's warning gave the Jews and the resistance three days to forestall the German plan.

'This proved absolutely vital to the success of the famous rescue operation,' Werner David Melchior, the student son of Denmark's acting Chief Rabbi, wrote twenty-five years later. 'This may well have been done with the explicit knowledge or tacit understanding of Dr Best, but once more Duckwitz was sticking out his neck very far, since in the event of the Gestapo's discovering the source of the leak, Dr Best would have washed his hands of it, and Duckwitz would have been made to bear the brunt of the wrath of the Party and the police.'

The Social Democrats alerted C. B. Henriques, the head of the Jewish community, who at first refused to believe them. Best had spread a fog of disinformation, signalling, via the Director-General of the Danish Foreign Ministry, Niels Svenningsen, and the Bishop of Copenhagen, Hans Fuglsang-Damgaard, that the Jews were safe. The Social Democrats also informed Rabbi Marcus Melchior, who, since the Chief Rabbi's arrest in August, was Denmark's most senior Jewish cleric still at liberty. Melchior was convinced that this latest warning was no idle rumour. The next day, 29 September, was the eve of Rosh Hashanah, the Jewish new year. The rabbi went to the synagogue for morning prayers and announced to his congregation that Rosh Hashanah services were cancelled and that the Jews were advised not to be in their homes during the next few days. They should await further developments. Despite the emergency and the absence of independent news media, the word spread swiftly along the grapevines of Copenhagen, the home of ninety-five per cent of Denmark's highly integrated, frequently intermarried, Jewish population.

Offers of help from friends, non-Jewish relatives and total strangers poured in. 'No rescue operation would have been possible', wrote Gerald Reitlinger, in his pioneer Holocaust history, *The Final Solution*, 'if the bulk of the Danish nation had not been sympathetic and a very large number of ordinary people disposed to risk their lives out of common charity.' A taxi driver was reported to have telephoned every Jewish name he could find in the directory. Richard Oestermann, a seventeen-year-old Jewish schoolboy, met a friend, a jazz drummer, in a Copenhagen street. 'I've just heard, the persecution of the Danish Jews will begin very soon,' the drummer told him. 'I must run. I have to spread the word.' Werner David Melchior went to the university to return some books and to leave a message for his professors. He was astonished at the reaction:

'Two students – I would meet them in the university doorways and exchange hellos, but we were not even studying together –

came up to me separately, on their own initiative, and said in more or less identical words, "Look, we know who you are. We hear all kinds of rumours. We don't know how much there is to them, but in case there is something that you think we might be able to do, for you or in general, our names are such and such. You'll find our addresses in the university catalogue. Get in touch in case of need." This happened to me twice in the ten minutes I spent at the university.'

The Jews were still not certain that the blow would fall, but they and their compatriots began to prepare the great escape. Rabbi Melchior sent Werner David across the sound to alert the Swedes. One of his friends, a businessman, had a secretary who was engaged to a fisherman. That was how contacts were made, casually and without central co-ordination. The fisherman and his partner agreed to ferry young Werner David and two other Jews across.

'I left the same evening by fishing boat [Werner David recalled]. There was room, apart from two fishermen, for three persons. The owners of the boat would not enter port. They were not sure yet whether the Swedes would confiscate the boat. So, at a distance from the coast, we found ourselves thrown into the water. Neither were the Swedes prepared to receive us. They did not know where to put us up, other than in the cells of the police station. There we remained in our wet clothes until morning.'

Eyvind Skjaer, a resistance activist and son of the Danish opera singer, Henry Skjaer, led Richard Oestermann, his ailing mother and two older sisters to a rendezvous with a fisherman named Andersen. They had agreed to pay him 1,000 crowns per person, a tidy sum, for ferrying them to Sweden. The Jews paid willingly. They knew the boatmen would lose their livelihoods if the craft were seized. It was about 9 p.m. on 1 October, the night the arrests began. Oestermann remembered crossing the coastal road and stealing down a tongue of land jutting into the sea:

'At the end of the tongue of land there was a wooden door, then a private anchorage. The door was locked. We were supposed to meet Andersen on the other side at ten o'clock. It was a misty evening, the fog was rolling, it was chilly. We could see Gestapo patrol cars going up and down the coast road. We heard the screams of Jews being caught. Eyvind and I looked at each other.

48

We said we'd better get going. We opened the lock with our bare hands. It was rusty and old, and I don't know how we did it. We got on the other side and closed the door behind us. We had a funny feeling that we were safe already. Ten o'clock came, then eleven o'clock. There was no boat. Then at midnight we heard the putter of an engine. It was Andersen.

'There was one other refugee on board, a Danish Communist. Andersen told my mother and sisters to go below deck. He gave me a blue fisherman's sweater and said, "You are my assistant. We must look as if we are out fishing." Then we set sail for Sweden. A German patrol boat approached with three men on board. I was dragging in the nets, making a big game of fishing. They turned away and we moved on to the Swedish island of Hven, but the fisherman said he was not going into port. The Swedes might confiscate his boat. He stuck an oar in the water and said, "One metre deep. This is where you get off. Jump!" We were still 50 or 100 metres from the shore. I jumped in first. It was more like one and a half metres deep. My family and the Communist followed. My sisters, who were strong swimmers, helped my mother. We half-swam, half-waded ashore. My shoes had come off and my feet were cut and bleeding. Up above us we saw two Swedish soldiers. They looked down at this forlorn little group and said, "Welcome to old Sweden." '

The soldiers took them across the island to an inn, where other refugees were assembled. 'We saw by the dozen the Jewish aristocracy of Copenhagen,' Oestermann told me. 'You had seen them a day or two before in all their elegance and confidence. Now you saw them as refugees with nothing. I myself was wearing three shirts. We had no luggage.'

Night after night for the next two weeks, hundreds of small boats followed them across to safety. Everybody knew somebody, who knew somebody. One Jew knew where other Jews were hiding. Almost the entire population co-operated, though one man, who was afraid, refused to shelter the Oestermann family in his beach house. What remained of public services and institutions played their part. No one was abandoned, but a 102-year-old Jewish woman remained concealed in Copenhagen until the liberation. Rabbi Melchior, his wife and four younger children, were sheltered by a Christian minister fifty miles outside the capital.

'One might say it was a matter of chance [argued Werner David], but repeated over and over again, these things ceased being matters of chance. My parents were sent on the next leg of the journey, southwards, to the island of Falster. The bishop there took care of my parents and participated, like his colleagues, in rescue work in general. The Danish police would occasionally seal off stretches of beach, where embarkations were taking place, pretending to search for illegal weapons, but in reality making passage safe from interference. In numerous instances, ambulances would drive the Jews to the beaches for embarkation. At the university, teachers and students went on a protest strike for three days. Many of these people anyhow were busily engaged in the rescue. Throughout three and a half years of occupation, there had never before been a time when the population stood as united behind the resistance.'

Inevitably, some boats were caught by German patrols. In one exceptional case, dozens of Jews awaiting embarkation were betrayed to the Gestapo. The 472 captives were transported to the Theresienstadt ghetto in Czechoslovakia. Even then, Denmark did not abandon them. Government and private agencies sent food parcels. In 1944, King Christian sent a mission to check how they were faring. About fifty of the Danish Jews perished.

Forty years later, Richard Oestermann, by then a foreign correspondent living and working in Israel, shipped one of the old rescue boats to Yad Vashem, where it is displayed next to the Avenue of the Righteous. It was a tiny skiff that carried a total of 200–300 Jews, Communists and shot-down Allied pilots into the deep waters of the sound, where they were picked up by fishing boats.

Georg Ferdinand Duckwitz remained at his post in Copenhagen, undetected and unpunished. He used his Danish contacts once again in 1944, this time to negotiate a compromise to a crippling strike. As a German untainted by war crimes, he stayed in the diplomatic service. On his first posting after 1945, he was warmly welcomed as West German Ambassador to Denmark.

• • •

Over five weeks in the early summer of 1940, Aristides de Sousa Mendes, the Portuguese Consul-General in Bordeaux, and his family signed entry visas for 30,000 refugees fleeing the Nazi occupation of France. About 10,000 of them were Jews, mainly from Belgium. Without Portuguese visas, they would not have been allowed to cross the border to the safety of neutral Spain. The Israeli historian, Yehuda Bauer, rated this operation as 'perhaps the largest rescue action by a single individual during the Holocaust'. The fifty-five-year-old, high-born Portuguese paid with his career, his pension and his not inconsiderable fortune. It took his family nearly half a century to shame Lisbon into rehabilitating him.

António de Oliveira Salazar, the absolute ruler of Portugal from 1933 to 1968, kept his country out of the war, but while Germany was still on an upward curve he was reluctant to provoke Hitler. Until May 1940, visa applications at the Bordeaux consulate-general, the nearest to the Spanish border, on the Quai Louis xviii were relayed by mail to Lisbon for a yea or a nay. The process was slow and cumbersome. Jewish applicants camped out in the yard of the local synagogue while they waited. At the beginning of May, the demand swelled so rapidly that the Consul-General had to wire the requests. Lisbon soon stopped answering. On 10 May, the Government banned further passage of refugees and instructed consuls in France not to issue visas to people who had no final destination and were seeking shelter in Portugal. No visas at all were to be issued to Jews. Mendes had to decide for himself: would he play the obedient bureaucrat, or would he take the risk of doing what his faith and conscience urged? Mendes, a devout Roman Catholic whose Jewish ancestors had converted to Christianity 400 years earlier, told his family that he felt driven by 'a divine power'. Visas would be issued free to all who needed them. According to his nephew, Cesar Mendes, 'He considered the pros and cons and decided to give all facilities without distinction of nationality, race or religion.'

The Consul-General was encouraged in his decision by a meeting with a Polish rabbi, Chaim Kruger, who was fleeing across France with his wife and five children. Kruger had been serving as rabbi of a Belgian congregation in Antwerp and spoke some French. One evening, the rabbi recounted, the Portuguese Consul-General's limousine drew up outside the synagogue yard. The rabbi and the diplomat fell into conversation, and Mendes invited the Krugers home to Quai Louis XVIII and offered the family shelter overnight:

'Our children were then between the ages of two and ten. The Consul-General told me he had thirteen children. He told us to make full use of all the amenities of his flat, but I had to explain that that would be impossible. I could not set myself apart from the large community of Jews who were milling around near the border. Also his home was full of [Christian] statues, which made a terrible impression on our children, who refused to eat a thing. I thanked him for his generosity. Next morning we returned to our milling brethren, and afterwards I went back to talk to him, to explain that there was just one way he could save us – by giving us visas to Portugal.

'In the middle of our discussion, the Vice-Consul overheard what I was saying and warned him not to fall into my net. All his efforts were to no avail. Mr Mendes told me that I and my family would receive visas. As for the other refugees, he would have to consult his ministry in Lisbon. I impressed upon him the need to ignore his assistant, and he told me that I could inform the refugees that anyone who wanted a visa could come and get it. I immediately announced this to the refugees. All of them received visas, and I aided him, stamping each visa, which he would then sign. He neither ate nor drank that whole day until late at night.'

Whether or not, as a fellow survivor was to suggest, the rabbi 'brought alive the dormant conscience of a Jew' in Mendes, he impressed him with the horror awaiting the fugitives if they fell into the hands of the Third Reich. 'I cannot allow these people to die,' the Consul-General's children remembered him saying. 'Our constitution says that the religion or the politics of a foreigner shall not be used to deny him refuge in Portugal. I have decided to follow this principle. Even if I am discharged, I can only act as a Christian, as my conscience tells me. If I am disobeying orders, I would rather be with God against men than with men against God.' David Shpiro, a Tel Aviv University researcher who is writing a book about Mendes, is convinced that the Consul-General was not at all motivated by his tenuous Jewish roots, though he made a point of mentioning them to Rabbi Kruger:

'He saw himself in no way as a Jew. He saw himself as a humane Christian. He was a devout Catholic, and he acted as a devout

Catholic. He knew that somewhere in his remote background there was someone who was a Jew, but like thousands of others in the Iberian peninsula that didn't make him a Jew. He saw himself as a Christian and a Portuguese patriot.'

Mendes, assisted by two of his children, Pedro and José, who were studying at Bordeaux University, and his music student nephew, Cesar, began issuing visas wholesale. Members of the Luxembourg royal family were among the non-Jewish recipients. Almost immediately, his Government ordered him to stop. Mendes turned a deaf ear and went on signing and stamping. As the Nazi conquerors fanned through France, the house on Quai Louis XVIII was awash with panic-stricken refugees. The Consul-General and his team worked from 8 a.m. to well past midnight. When they ran out of official stationery, they used any piece of paper that came to hand. Cesar, now retired after a career as a violinist, described the chaos:

'The dining-room, the drawing-room and the Consul's offices were at the disposal of the refugees, dozens of them of both sexes, all ages, and mainly old and sick people. They were coming and going. There were pregnant women who did not feel well; there were people who had seen, powerless to defend themselves, their relatives die on the highways, killed by machine-guns firing from 'planes. They slept on chairs, on the floor, on the rugs. Everything was out of control. Even the Consul's offices were crowded with dozens of refugees, who were exhausted, dead tired, because they had waited for days and nights on the street, on the stairways and finally in the offices. They could not satisfy their needs, they did not eat or drink for fear of losing their place in the queues, but this happened nevertheless and caused some disturbances. Consequently, the refugees looked bad: they did not wash themselves, they did not comb their hair, they did not change their clothes and they did not shave. Most of them had nothing but the clothes they were wearing. The incidents took on such proportions that it was necessary to ask the army to preserve order. In each room and in each office there was a soldier. These soldiers were under the orders of a sergeant. In the chancellery, they worked all day long and part of the night. My uncle got ill, exhausted, and had to lie down.'

Cesar remembered a French political refugee, a professor at the

Sorbonne, who moved into his uncle's house. He ate with the family in the kitchen (the dining-room having been surrendered to the fugitives) and slept in one of the bedrooms. 'This gentleman never removed his pyjamas from the night he first came in, the same night that Bordeaux was bombed and 500 people were killed. He lived in terror of being taken by the Nazis. His fear was justified because he had written against Hitler's regime. His fortune was quite large and consisted of pure gold in four potato sacks. To induce my uncle to grant him a visa, he promised him half of his fortune. My uncle rejected the offer, but granted him the visa.'

Bordeaux was bombed on the night of 20 June. Two days later, France signed an armistice with Germany. The Portuguese Foreign Ministry feared for the Mendes family's safety. The Consul-General was relieved of his post, and two officials arrived with a car to take them home. Mendes complied, but was not yet finished. During a stopover in Bayonne, he was dismayed to find that the Portuguese Vice-Consul was turning away refugees. He angrily issued hundreds of visas of his own. At the border town of Hendaye, he picked up another band of fugitives, who were worried that Spain was about to close the frontier. He improvised handwritten visas, then instructed them to walk behind his car through a rarely used crossing-point, where the single guard had no telephone and no way of checking with his superiors. The bluff worked. The refugees shuffled to safety.

Aristides de Sousa Mendes was less fortunate. The Foreign Ministry dismissed him for disobedience after thirty years' service and cancelled his pension rights. He remained unrepentant. During a brief reunion in Lisbon at this time, he told Rabbi Kruger, 'If thousands of Jews are to suffer because of one Catholic [Hitler], it was worth it for one Catholic to suffer for all the Jews.' At fifty-five and disgraced, he was unable to find work. He was barred from practising law, which he had studied before entering the diplomatic service. He appealed to the national assembly after the war, but was snubbed. Bit by bit he sold everything he had, including the family estate in the mountain town of Cabanas de Viriato. Four decades later, the land is worked by a local farmer, but the forty-five-roomed château has fallen into ruins. Enterprising neighbours now sell the heroic Consul-General's abandoned books and family papers to tourists as souvenirs. Mendes's wife,

Angelina, who had shared the moral burden in the Quai Louis XVIII, died after a stroke in 1948. Mendes died, impoverished and unnoticed, six years later.

Led by one of his sons, Sebastian, who had settled in the United States, the children took up the struggle for a posthumous rehabilitation, but drew no response until after Salazar was overthrown in 1968. Even then, it was six more years before the new, democratic regime agreed to review the case. A former ambassador, Dr Nuno de Bessa Lopes, found in 1976, after a two-year investigation, that Mendes had been wrongfully dismissed and recommended that his honour be restored. Among the Foreign Ministry papers he dredged up was one referring to the Mendes family as 'descendants of Jews'. Someone had evidently concluded that he saved Jews because he was one himself. 'Apparently,' Lopes wrote, 'the poor Consul Sousa Mendes was unable to escape the claws of the new Inquisition, which stubbornly persists in Portugal.' As if to prove his point, Lopes's report was suppressed for another decade.

It was only in 1986, under persistent pressure from the Mendes family, backed by the Portuguese media, that the Socialist President, Mario Soares, bestowed the Order of Liberty medal posthumously on the disobedient Consul-General. Soares, who received American-based members of the family at the Portuguese Embassy in Washington, acknowledged, 'There is an old saying in Portugal that we honour the best of our sons very poorly.' As the *Los Angeles Times* reported: 'That left his memory in a new kind of limbo – honoured, but not yet restored.' The campaign soldiered on until finally, on 18 March 1988, the national assembly unanimously adopted a bill reinstating Mendes to full rank in the consular corps and compensating the family financially.

The Lisbon daily paper, *Diario de Noticias*, commented, 'It was the duty of a democracy towards the man who constitutes one of the most authentic symbols of the generosity, tolerance and human compassion of the Portuguese spirit. He had already been rehabilitated in our hearts, but this formal rehabilitation was overdue and an imperative for our country.' Sebastian Mendes, by then a sixty-four-year-old retired postal worker living in California, said, 'I can now sleep in peace because what I started forty-five years ago has finally been successful.'

• • •

'How one regrets the anonymity of these Red Cross reports,' bemoaned Gerald Reitlinger in his account of the liberation of the Mauthausen concentration camp. Happily for later writers, the staid International Committee of the Red Cross has since lifted its self-imposed embargo, albeit slowly, albeit reluctantly. The ICRC is a private, Swiss-based organization dedicated to monitoring the application and development of international humanitarian law. It works discreetly. It believes in talking to governments and it is careful not to interfere in their internal affairs. Countless victims of conflict in four continents have reason to be grateful for its persistent, but tactful, intervention. But the Second World War was no ordinary conflict, the Jews of Europe were no ordinary victims. Once the enormity of Hitler's Final Solution became known, Geneva bent its own rules, but it did not break them. Red Cross lawyers sought legal cover for every extension of foreign operations. Head office debated, defined and sent instructions to its delegates in the field. It was not indifferent to the suffering of the Jews, but it was inhibited by a fear of jeopardizing other Red Cross operations.

Life in the lands under Nazi occupation was less orderly. The ICRC's Swiss delegates could not always stick to the book, though some tried harder than others. Two mavericks, who between them saved thousands of Jews in the disintegrating final months of the war, waited a long time for recognition. Like the consuls, they bluffed, threatened and risked their reputations, if not their lives. Diplomatic immunity was no guarantee. The Polish Chargé d'Affaires in Budapest, Henryk Slawik, was executed at Mauthausen after issuing thousands of documents certifying that Polish Jewish refugees were Christians (he put 100 children in a Catholic orphanage, where they were taught Judaism during the week and taken to church on Sunday). Raoul Wallenberg was warned that 'accidents' could happen, even to protected foreigners. He was not alone in such danger. The Red Cross men did not always wait to clear their initiatives with Geneva. They responded to the needs of the day, the hour and the moment. They improvised. Above all, they did not give up.

Louis Haefliger, a forty-year-old volunteer sent on an errand of mercy to Mauthausen at the end of April 1945, two weeks before the capitulation of the Thousand-Year Reich, committed the unforgivable sin of compromising Swiss neutrality. He led American tanks into the Austrian camp, 100 miles west of Vienna, to prevent the SS guards from carrying out orders to blow it up with its 50,000 remaining inmates. Mauthausen, commemorated in a ballad by the Greek composer Mikis Theodorakis, was a slave labour camp. It worked and starved its prisoners to death. The *Encyclopaedia of the Holocaust* estimated that almost 200,000 passed through it between 1939 and 1945. Of these, 119,000 died. Some ninety-five per cent of the deaths were from starvation or diseases caused by starvation. Many of the inmates were political prisoners or other 'undesirables', some of them Jews. Larger groups of Jews were sent there from the middle of 1944. They were singled out for even harsher treatment than the others. More than 38,000 Jews died in Mauthausen. When Haefliger arrived at its gates, it was still (in Reitlinger's phrase) 'the atrocity camp par excellence'. Little had changed since an earlier Red Cross visitor reported that 'something mysterious and horrible hovered over everything'.

Mauthausen owed much of its horror to Standartenführer Franz Ziereis, a baby-faced sadist who commanded it from August 1939 to May 1945. The SS major thought nothing of shooting thirty or forty prisoners a day in the back of the neck. He boasted to Haefliger that he had once ordered a truck loaded with corpses to be driven to the front of his villa to show his wife how busy he had been. Haefliger's mission was to secure the release of Allied citizens in the camp and to distribute food parcels to the other inmates. On the way from Switzerland, he came upon a forced march of emaciated Russian prisoners of war. SS guards shot anyone who fell by the wayside. 'Murder, cold-blooded murder right in front of my eyes,' Haefliger wrote three decades later. 'I felt like jumping out of my car and throttling those SS men, but my driver held me back.' He carried his anger with him to Mauthausen.

The Red Cross official first demonstrated his independence by insisting that he be allowed to supervise distribution of food parcels without discrimination to all the inmates. This would also ensure that he could see for himself what was happening inside the camp. He found Ziereis unexpectedly responsive. The commandant could hear the sound of Allied bombing and artillery fire, and a character witness might yet be useful. Haefliger was billeted in the SS barracks, where he spotted an order to destroy everything before the Allies got there. He tried to persuade the commandant to cancel it, but with qualified success. Ziereis agreed that the Red Cross man could write at the bottom of the order: 'Cancelled according to verbal instructions by Standartenführer Ziereis, signed Haefliger.' The major was in a state of emotional collapse, and the Red Cross man could not predict what the outcome would be. 'By now', Haefliger wrote, 'I was completely indifferent to my own fate. I only wanted to do something for the prisoners.'

He therefore took the law into his own hands. He instructed prisoners in the camp tailor's shop to make two flags, one white for surrender, one with the red cross of the ICRC. He told other prisoners in the camp garage to paint an SS Opel in neutral white, and persuaded his Nazi room-mate, a Lieutenant Reiner, to rip the SS insignia off his uniform. On 5 May, the Red Cross delegate and the Nazi officer drove off in the white Opel to look for the advancing Allies. Eventually, they encountered three American tanks. Haefliger struggled to explain in rudimentary English who he was and what he wanted. One of the young GIs interrupted, 'You can speak German to me. I'm Jewish and I was born in Vienna.' Haefliger urged them to free Mauthausen and its two satellite camps before the SS destroyed them and slaughtered the surviving inmates. The American divisional commander gave his approval, and the white Opel led an armoured column to liberate the death camps. The Germans put up no resistance and the prisoners hoisted the white and Red Cross flags. The baby-faced commandant fled into the woods, but was betrayed by one of his own sons and was shot attempting to escape.

In his native Switzerland, Louis Haefliger remained one of Reitlinger's anonymous Red Cross men for more than thirty years, though he was awarded a medal by resistance veterans in Austria, where he eventually made his home. Whenever he applied for a job in Switzerland, he was turned down. 'I always read between the lines that they considered me unreliable, an adventurer,' he told Ernie Meyer, of the *Jerusalem Post*, when the city of Jerusalem honoured him in 1980. ' "What business is it of yours?" was the prevailing attitude then. It has only slowly changed now.' None the less, he never protested when he was ostracized by the Red Cross establishment: 'I know I overstepped its guidelines and acted against Swiss neutrality by summoning the American armed forces to Mauthausen. But I acted according to my conscience.'

Friedrich Born, another unsung Red Cross hero, was not given his due until 1987, twenty-four years after his death. Even his son and daughter knew nothing of his exploits as the ICRC's chief delegate in Budapest before a Tel Aviv lawyer, Arieh Ben-Tov, published a doctoral thesis on the Red Cross and the Jews of Hungary. Born was not disgraced. He was simply ignored. Geneva was so uneasy about his liberal interpretation of his mandate that it twice sent colleagues to work alongside him. It is hard to avoid the conclusion that their main task was to keep him in line.

Born, a former chairman of the Swiss chamber of commerce in Budapest, was sent back by the Red Cross in May 1944. In the declining months of Miklós Horthy's pro-German regency, Jews were already being deported en masse, ostensibly to forced labour, in fact to the gas chambers of Auschwitz. Since Hungary was still in theory independent, under Horthy and the Arrow Cross Fascists who overthrew him, Geneva constantly reminded the delegation to keep out of its internal affairs. The ultimate form of this doctrine would have been that what the Hungarian Government did to Hungarian Jews was no one else's business. Geneva opted for a softer version. At about the same time that Born was unpacking his bags in Budapest, four young Jews escaped from Auschwitz and reported on the grim reality of industrialized extermination. From 15 May, they said, trains were delivering 12,000 Jews a day from Hungary. From the 'selection' platform, SS doctors sent more than eighty-five per cent of them straight to the gas chambers, which were operating around the clock. In the light of these revelations, the Red Cross authorized its man in Budapest to help Jews as best he could, but hoped he would not stray too far outside his brief.

André Durand, the historian of the ICRC, wrote of Born's performance:

The ICRC delegate did what he could to help those in danger. He protested against the brutal treatment of Jews, obtained a decree from the Ministry of the Interior forbidding looting, gave asylum to members of the Jewish Council in Budapest and obtained the right of extraterritoriality for the buildings occupied by the ICRC delegation. He organized food supplies to the ghetto, health examination and accommodation for children.

But Geneva was watching and worrying. Head office did not like the fact that Born protested at the ill-treatment of individuals as well as of groups. There were misgivings about the multiplicity of buildings on which he conferred Red Cross protection. Reflecting the conventional wisdom within the organization, Born's deputy, Hans Weyermann, complained that the delegate had granted protection to 'innumerable hospitals and public service buildings (water and gas works, fire stations, etc.) and thousands of private properties', all with ICRC plaques. It was, he argued, an illusion to think that any army would respect such large numbers of buildings. Born created and expanded a Jewish affairs department within his office, hiring hundreds of Jews and protecting them from deportation. He looked after 7,000 children in sixty institutions. He retrieved 7,500 out of 50,000 Jews earmarked for the transports, sometimes using his own car to bring them back from the railhead. At one point he accepted a request from the abbot of a twelfth-century Benedictine monastery to place it under Red Cross protection. Although it was in the war zone, the Germans respected its immunity. About 1,000 Jewish and half-Jewish children were given shelter there. Conservative estimates suggest that Friedrich Born and the ICRC saved about 11,000 Jews.

Arieh Ben-Tov, himself a Polish survivor of Auschwitz, admired Born's courage and priorities, while acknowledging that the Red Cross purists had a point:

What Born did must be considered as private initiative, since in strictly legal terms the Geneva Convention covered only the military victims of the war. It was only after the Second World War that the protection of the conventions was extended to civilian war victims. Born adopted an extensive interpretation of his humanitarian mission which went beyond the instructions from Geneva. Given the events of the time, the fact that for thousands of people the protection of the ICRC was the only way to avoid evacuation from Budapest, and given that many of these people wished to defy the scorched-earth policy and save their city, Born's behaviour is understandable and accords completely with moral principles even if it fails to comply with purely legal constraints.

After publication of Ben-Tov's critical work, the International Red Cross commissioned an independent Swiss study of its record. The upshot was an overdue vindication of Born's initiative in Budapest and Haefliger's in Mauthausen. The Director-General, Jacques Moreillon, wrote in August 1988:

One can say, with hindsight, that in some countries where the domination of the Third Reich was not total, the ICRC could probably have saved more Jewish people than it did. In those countries, the ICRC today feels that it did not seek out, at that time, all the possible means of protecting more of the victims. . . .

The ICRC of today reiterates its gratitude to all those delegates who, under the banner of the Red Cross, discovered how to take effective action and save tens of thousands of lives, often at their own peril, not only during the war but also when some of the concentration camps were liberated.

3

Prisoners' Prisoners

It was the Germans who dubbed Charles Coward the 'Count of Auschwitz'. They must have regretted ever taking the restless Cockney sergeant-major prisoner. For five years, from 1940 to 1945, he conducted an ingenious one-man campaign of subversion and subterfuge, bribery and corruption, against the Nazi war effort. He escaped, and was recaptured, nineteen times. He smuggled arms and explosives for the Polish resistance. Prisoners of war working under his command systematically sabotaged production. Consignments of sugar from a forced-labour refinery mysteriously caught fire in transit. Newly installed power cables developed inexplicable fractures. In his coded letters home, he relayed valuable information to British intelligence. Coward, the ultimate barrack-room lawyer, knew the Hague and Geneva Conventions better than his captors and, as liaison with the International Red Cross, never missed an opportunity to torment the Germans with chapter and verse. A professional soldier, who had joined the Royal Artillery twenty years earlier and seen service in India, he was in his late thirties, a big brother if not a father figure to his fellow prisoners. They deferred to his experience as much as to his rank.

It was in the Monowitz POW camp, about a mile from Auschwitz, that Coward came face to face with the pitiless brutality of the Third Reich – and resolved to fight it. British prisoners were digging trenches and laying cables to one of the Auschwitz factories. Reynolds, a young corporal, refused to climb a pylon in the freezing Polish winter without rubber boots and thick gloves. A furious German guard ordered him to go up. When Reynolds walked away, protesting that it would be suicidal, the guard drew a revolver and shot him dead. 'This was the last straw,' Coward's biographer, John Castle, wrote, 'the final seal on his contempt and detestation of Germans.' At about the same time, Coward returned from visiting a neighbouring town on Red Cross business and witnessed the arrival and 'selection' of a trainload of Jews, dispatched either to slave labour or directly to the gas chambers and glowing crematoria. His German escort rejoiced that they were walking to their deaths. The pathetic parade reinforced Coward's animosity.

His first dealings with the Jewish inmates came when he smuggled dynamite into Auschwitz for the resistance. He made the most of his relatively free access as Red Cross liaison and Allied prisoners' spokesman – and of the bribery value of his POW food parcels. During one of these missions he plotted what must rank as the most ghoulish of all Holocaust rescue operations, a trade of corpses for contraband, the living for the dead.

Coward struck a bargain with a venal sergeant-major, who was in charge of an emaciated gang of Jewish workers. On agreed dates, the German delivered the bodies of three Jews who had died of disease and exhaustion. He was paid in cigarettes and chocolate, coffee and soap, donated by Coward's POWs. Coward then tipped off his Jewish resistance contact, a Hungarian lawyer who spoke English. He in turn briefed three inmates to prepare to escape. Coward had noticed that batches of labourers, starved and no longer fit to work, were marched every night from Auschwitz to the gas chambers in the twin Birkenau camp. They were already more than half dead, and the German guards at the beginning and the end of the column hardly noticed if some perished by the wayside. They would be collected later.

With the help of another POW, 'Tich' Keenan, Coward hid his three stiffening corpses in a ditch that ran along the road from Auschwitz to Birkenau. The three condemned men chosen by the Hungarian lawyer placed themselves inconspicuously in the centre of the 200 or so marchers, dropping out according to plan. Coward beckoned them into the ditch, then scattered the three bodies along the roadside for the Germans to find. The book-keeping would tally. He and Keenan gave the men clothes to replace their striped concentration camp pyjamas and told them to hoof it into the forest. There were no promises, but they were at least given a chance to live. The macabre commerce was repeated many times over the next few months until warnings reached Coward that the Gestapo was on his trail. In a vain search for another Jewish victim – a British army doctor, taken prisoner but treated as a Jew rather than a POW – Coward once switched identities with a Jewish inmate and spent a night in a verminous Auschwitz barracks.

One of Coward's fellow POWs was Yitzhak Perski, a Jewish sergeant from Palestine, father of the future Israeli Prime Minister and Labour leader, Shimon Peres. Perski, a Polish-born timber merchant already in his early forties, had volunteered for the Royal Engineers and served with the Eighth Army in North Africa and Greece before he was captured. Like Coward, he was an inveterate escaper. It was Perski, as a member of the Monowitz escape committee, who collected the cigarettes and chocolate for bribing the Germans. On one occasion he saved Coward from execution. The sergeant-major was caught digging an escape tunnel and was about to be sentenced to death. Perski, who had been steadily bribing the commandant, threatened to expose him if Coward were punished. The commandant decided to give him another chance.

Coward and Perski escaped together three or four times, from Monowitz and other camps. Once, disguised as Bulgarian labourers going home on leave, they reached the Swiss border, but Coward's cockney accent gave them away. Twenty years later, when Coward stayed with Perski in Tel Aviv, the two old soldiers were still arguing about whose fault it was. They first met in Greece, when both were on the run. A resistance fighter took Perski to the village of Lamia, near Mount Olympus, where Coward was organizing an assorted group of about twenty escaped British and Australian prisoners. They hired an open boat and rowed from the Peloponnese towards neutral Turkey. It was very cold and the men had no food. One of the soldiers died and Coward removed his stripes and assumed his identity. But the boat was spotted by a German seaplane. Before they were recaptured, Coward ordered his men to raise one hand and swear not to divulge the Jewish identity of Perski and one or two others. Perski believed that he might have been executed there and then if the secret had come out. On a later occasion, Coward reprimanded a Scottish POW who shouted 'Jew' at him.

While they were being shuttled from camp to camp, the group planned to escape from a train. They acquired a file and a saw, but were discovered at the last minute. The German officer in charge of the party held Perski and another British POW responsible and sentenced them to death. Perski told of being stripped naked and taken to the side of the track for summary execution:

'Charlie Coward and the group demanded that a priest, who was also a prisoner, be called to receive the last confessions of the condemned men. They told the priest that one of us was a Jew, and that he must protect and try to save him. So the priest, who arrived in the nick of time, threatened and cajoled and succeeded in persuading the Nazi officer to postpone the execution until we got back to the prison camp, where a proper investigation and trial would be held. The priest even declared that if we were killed, the officer would have to kill him as well. We were returned to the train and continued on to the prison camp.'

No one can know how many Jews Coward saved from Auschwitz, or how many of them reached the underground and survived the war. In his book, *The Password Is Courage*, John Castle put the figure at nearly 400. Gershon Peres, Yitzhak Perski's second son, believed it might be as high as 700 or 800. When Coward, a dapper, bow-tied figure with Brylcreemed hair parted down the middle, stayed with his old comrade in Arba Aratzot Street, Tel Aviv, in 1962, hundreds of survivors who had read that the 'Count' was in town gathered outside the house and presented him with an inscribed gold watch. When Gershon asked him why he had risked his life to save Jews, Coward insisted that he had done nothing special. 'He was humble, simple and straight,' Gershon told me. 'He was a charming gentleman, a man without ambition.'

After being transferred from Auschwitz at the beginning of 1945, Coward was liberated by the advancing Americans in the middle of his final escape. He went home to his wife and two children in Edmonton, a North London industrial suburb, where he worked in a factory. When he was invited to Israel to receive a medal from the President, his Jewish employers refused to give him paid leave, though other Jewish businessmen were more generous when the story became public. His last job was in the dispatch department of an Oxford Street store. He died of cancer in 1976.

Coward returned twice to Germany, in 1947 as a key witness in the trial of twenty-five directors of I. G. Farben, a major employer of slave labour at Auschwitz, and to testify in a 1953 damages suit brought against the giant chemical combine by a Jewish survivor. The plaintiff, Norbert Wollheim, was awarded 10,000 marks in a verdict that opened the way for thousands of similar claims. The German judges commended Coward's moral courage in daring to help the Jewish prisoners. 'He did this', they wrote, 'for the mere reason that he and the prisoners were fellow human beings.' The court contrasted this with the conduct of I. G. Farben, who 'did not look upon the Jewish prisoners as people entitled to the rights of human beings, or else did not or could not muster the moral courage they were obliged to show as employers'. The judgment concluded: 'The fact that a British prisoner of war had to show the German defendants what moral courage involved is a matter of regret to a German court.'

• • •

It was Adélaïde Hautval's indignation at the Nazis' dehumanizing of Jews that got her into Auschwitz in the first place. Dr Hautval was a thirty-six-year-old French psychiatrist, the daughter of a Protestant pastor from Alsace-Lorraine. She was working in a clinic in the south-west when the Germans occupied France. In April 1942, she learned that her mother had died. The clinic was in the occupied zone, but her mother's home in the lower Rhine was still under French rule. She applied for a permit to cross from one zone to the other. When it was refused, she tried to get there without papers, but was caught in the demarcation zone. She was waiting for a train on a station platform at Bourges when she saw some Germans ill-treating a Jewish family. She intervened and told them in German to leave them in peace. 'But don't you see,' one of the Germans asked, 'they're only Jews?' The doctor retorted, 'So what? They are people like any others, leave them alone.' The Gestapo clapped her in the local jail.

Soon after her arrival, a number of Jewish prisoners were brought in. A Jewish woman was placed in the doctor's cell. When she saw that the woman had been forced to wear a yellow star, Dr Hautval made herself a similar star out of paper and complained to the Gestapo that French Jews were being treated like inferior beings. Many things, she said, were denied them. They were barred from travelling on the Metro. On ordinary trains, they had to ride in the rear compartments. Her jailers were furious, but offered to release her if she retracted. 'But why should I say anything different? The Jews are people like any others,' the doctor replied. 'Since you wish to defend them,' a Gestapo officer snapped, 'you will share their fate!'

For the next nine months the dissenting doctor was shuttled around France from one Jewish prison camp to another. The Gestapo forced her to stitch a Star of David on her coat together with a band reading: 'A friend of the Jews'. As camp doctor, she often had to calm Jewish patients who feared that she was about to inject them with lethal doses. 'It took me a long time', she wrote later, 'before I understood.' In January 1943, she was sent with a trainload of 230 French women political prisoners, mostly Communists, to Auschwitz, a three-day journey by cattle truck into the hell of occupied Poland. The first thing they saw was an electrified fence stretching to the horizon. In defiance, the women sang the 'Marseillaise' as they were marched in the morning mist to their barracks through a cordon of German soldiers and guard dogs. The number 31802 was tattooed on her arm. Within three months, 160 of the 230 were dead. Dr Hautval was suffering from corrosive ulcers on her legs.

It was at this time that Dr Edward Wirths, a Nazi doctor, visited her and asked whether she would like to practise gynaecology. It was a strange question to ask a psychiatrist. Dr Hautval had heard rumours that Auschwitz doctors were conducting sterilization experiments. Her suspicions were aroused, and she asked Dr Wirths what kind of work he had in mind. The doctor refused to answer, which only deepened her misgivings, but thinking that one day she might get out of the concentration camp and report on what was going on there, Dr Hautval accepted the invitation, though she knew that she was playing 'a dangerous game'.

Soon afterwards, she was transferred from the women's quarters at Birkenau to the main Auschwitz camp. Ten Jewish women were moved with her to the notorious Block 10, where, in the words of the novelist Leon Uris, 'the raw material for the human experiments was kept imprisoned'. It was a rough, two-storey building with planks nailed across the windows. About 100 Jewish women, mostly French and Greek, were incarcerated there when Dr Hautval arrived. During her stay, the number rose to 400 or 500, with successive convoys bringing in reinforcements from France, Belgium, Holland, Slovakia and Germany. Apart from an Austrian woman recuperating from typhus, Dr Hautval was the only Christian in Block 10. One convoy of women from Birkenau brought typhus with them. Fearing that they would be killed, Dr Hautval hid them on the top floor of the block and treated them as best she could. 'None of us are going to get out of this alive,' she told a fellow prisoner, 'but so long as we are here we must behave like human beings.'

Dr Wirths and his brother, an SA stormtrooper officer who called himself a gynaecologist, told her that they were seeking a cure for cancer of the uterus. She did some internal examinations for them to explore the pre-cancerous stages and was surprised at the high incidence of disease. Suspecting that this was no coincidence, she confided in another doctor, who advised her to keep her suspicions to herself. Instead, she told Dr Wirths that she could not continue with the examinations. He ordered her next to work with Professor Karl Clauberg, director of a gynaecological clinic in Silesia, on his sterilization programme. Dr Hautval refused to have anything to do with Clauberg, whom she remembered as 'a small, bald civilian who sported a Tyrolean hat and ski boots'. His 'research' entailed injecting caustic fluid into the uterus, which Dr Hautval reported later 'caused atrocious suffering for many of the women'.

When Dr Wirths's brother, a man with grey-blue 'romantic' eyes, sought her views on sterilization, Dr Hautval decided that a straight question deserved a straight answer. 'I am absolutely opposed,' she replied. When the German expressed surprise that a doctor practising psychiatry should oppose a selection procedure aimed at preserving the race, she answered that the whole business was highly debatable and, in any case, was open to abuse. The SA officer tried to justify the experiments by arguing that, after all, the patients were 'only' Jews. Dr Hautval retorted, 'We have no right to dispose of the life and destiny of others.' The

Nazis thought again about sending Dr Hautval to help with the sterilizations.

She did, however, examine some Jewish girls in Block 10 who had been irradiated in these experiments. It was not easy to get access to them. The Nazi doctors were competing to have these patients for their researches. The prestige to be gained was so high that several of them often 'looked after' the same woman. One of these guinea pigs, who survived the war, was examined by a British medical officer. He reported that she was thirty-five, but 'looked at least twenty years older'. The authorities bullied Dr Hautval to anaesthetize two Greek Jewish girls, aged seventeen or eighteen, whose ovaries were being removed by a Dr Samuel, a privileged German Jewish prisoner, whom Dr Hautval described as 'overwhelmed by fear and a desire to please the authorities', and who, for all his efforts, was eventually taken out and shot.

The operations, carried out simultaneously, took about half an hour. The next time the French doctor was asked to give an anaesthetic, she refused and Dr Samuel denounced her to Dr Wirths. Dr Hautval reported the ensuing, electrifying exchange to a court of the Queen's Bench in London twenty years later:

'Dr Wirths called me to him. He asked me whether it was true that I had refused both the operation and to give the anaesthetic. I said it was true. He asked me why, and I answered him that it was contrary to my principles as a doctor. He asked me, "You cannot see that these people are different from you?" I answered that there were lots of other people different from me, starting with him.'

Instead of being punished, the French doctor was sent back to Birkenau and advised to keep out of sight. After the liberation, she returned to her practice in France, where she died in 1988. Her story came to light in 1964, when a Polish doctor who had taken part in the Auschwitz experiments, Wladyslaw Alexander Dering, sued Leon Uris for libel. Dr Hautval was called to testify that it was possible to say 'No' in Auschwitz and survive. The judge, Mr Justice Lawton, commended her as 'one of the most impressive and courageous women who has ever given evidence in the courts of this country'. She had, he added, stood up to the Nazis four times and made it quite clear what she was and what she was not prepared to do. The 'devastating reply' she gave to Dr Wirths, the

Judge said, would 'live in the jury's memory for many years'. Dr Dering, who had settled in London and was practising medicine in Seven Sisters Road, won the case, but was awarded derisory damages of one halfpenny. Dr Hautval had made her point.

When she was informed in March 1965 that Israel was awarding her the Medal of the Righteous, she replied that the title was reserved for God alone and not for mortals. She added, 'What I did was perfectly natural, logical and derived from a moral obligation.' Leon Uris, author of *Exodus* and *QB VII*, had the last word: 'If we had had more friends like Dr Hautval, there could never have been a Nazi era.'

• • •

The British prisoners of war, working-class provincial boys captured during the evacuation from Dunkirk, had hardly met a Jew before. If they thought hard, they might remember the odd soldier who was excused church parade. Until a bleak, icy day in January 1945, they knew nothing of the murderous brutality of Hitler's Final Solution. They had spent most of the previous five years in a time warp, labouring on farms in the obscure, German-speaking Polish border village of Gross Golemkau, south of what was then Danzig and is now Gdansk. 'We didn't know the words concentration camp,' one of them confessed. They were jolted out of their ignorance in the last winter of the war by a squad of SS men driving 300 living skeletons through the village, the frail survivors of 1,200 Jewish women force-marched west because their jailers needed a pretext to escape the advancing Red Army. One of the POWs among the gaggle of peasants turning out to watch the pathetic procession was Willie Fisher, who kept a diary. That night he wrote in anger:

They came straggling through the bitter cold, about 300 of them, limping, dragging footsteps, slipping and falling, to rise and stagger under the blows of the guards – SS swine. Crying loudly for bread, screaming for food, 300 matted-haired filthy objects that had once been Jewesses.

One of the marchers was Sara Matuson, a sixteen-year-old Lithuanian girl, who had set out six weeks earlier with her mother and older sister from the Stutthoff death camp. The women walked all day and slept at night in any barn the guards could find – packed so tight that Sara remembered it four decades later as 'standing-room only':

'Most of us were dressed in thin rayon dresses with short sleeves and a big red Star of David painted on the back. I had a thin spring coat, clogs and a blanket. From the blanket you made rags for your feet. You put it over your head as a shawl. We hardly got any food. We were so hungry we ate the snow on the road. If a farmer had cooked something, we got food. Once a German guard gave me a slice of bread. My mother slept on it, but someone stole it during the night. Once we got potato peel and manure a farmer had cooked for his pigs. People used to dig for roots. They were shot on the spot. You were so hungry, you risked being shot. We'd covered about 200 kilometres. Women who couldn't walk were shot. Others died from hunger, others froze. It was very cold. My mother's fingers froze. She couldn't even pull down her pants any more. We had flannel pants.'

Sara was still fighting for life. Her mother, Gita, the wife of a once prosperous leather-factory owner, had managed to keep a diamond ring. As they entered Gross Golemkau, Sara asked her to hand it over so that she could try and barter it for bread.

'I slipped out of the line – don't ask how, I don't know how – and into a ditch. I ran into a barn. A man came in. I said, "Here's a ring, bring me bread." He took it, but came back with the police, who said, "What are you doing?" I replied, "I came to get bread." I showed that I came from the march. They shouted, "You are dirtying our *Judenfrei* town." A whole posse started chasing me. Before you knew it, it was a mob chasing me back towards the march. I said to myself, "I don't mind if they kill me, but not in front of my mother." People were standing on the roadside. I forced them aside and ran into a barn. It was animal instinct. I laid myself in a trough. There were cows in the barn. They looked for me – the police and the others – for two hours, but didn't find me.'

The hue and cry petered out, then a man came into the barn. Sara asked him in German, 'Are you Polish?' He answered, 'No, I'm British.' The man was one of the POWs, Stan Wells, who had served in the Royal Norfolk Regiment. He reassured her in rudimentary German that he knew she was the runaway Jewish girl and that the police had stopped looking for her.

'I felt pity [he recalled]. I was sorry for her. She was in such a state. Ragged, very thin, crying. That's how I found her: I heard her sobbing. I told her to lie still and keep quiet. I made sure she was safe. I had to leave her for the time being.'

Sara remembered Wells giving her a hunk of bread, which she wolfed down. He explained that he lived in a makeshift jail with nine other British prisoners. They were working for different farmers. He knew a Russian girl from a nearby forced labour camp. Wells promised to ask the girl to find Sara shelter. If she refused, the POWs would see what they could do. In any case, he would come back the next day. Before leaving, Wells hid a lantern which the farmer's wife used when she checked the cows during the night. It was as well that he did. Around midnight, Sara heard someone come into the barn:

'I stayed in the trough. The farmer's wife couldn't find the lamp. She groped around in the dark. She touched my leg. "Who's there? Who's there?" she called. I didn't say a word. She shook me, then she went out. I didn't even budge. I was letting fate take its course. I felt so sorry for myself. My father must have been watching over me.'

In the morning, the farmer's wife told Wells that she had found an army deserter sleeping in the barn. 'I wanted to bring him into the house,' she said. Wells had mixed news for Sara. The women in the Russian girl's camp would not take the Jewish fugitive, but Wells had talked to his fellow POWs and they had agreed to hide her. They remembered that when they were taken prisoner and were marched through Holland on their way to Germany, Dutch townsfolk had risked being shot to throw food to them.

By now, Sara was sick with diarrhoea from not eating. When Willie Fisher came to fetch her, she was at first afraid of him. For some reason, she thought that he was drunk. But he gave her an army greatcoat and a cap, instructed her on how to behave so that she would not arouse suspicion, and then marched her boldly through the village to their barracks.

The POWs knew that they were taking a risk. 'We were aware that any indiscipline was punishable,' Stan Wells told me in March 1989. 'We were aware of the chances we took, but they didn't come into it. At that time things were getting desperate. Anything could have happened. It was just the chance we took. It came to me that we had a place to put her, and everybody was in agreement.' Two other POWs, Alan Edwards and George Hammond, concurred:

'It didn't matter to us that she was Jewish. She was just a human being. If she had been Polish or any other nationality, we would have done the same. Perhaps not if she was German. She had to have some help or she would have died. We didn't debate it very long. We all sat round the table and discussed it. We got an idea to put her in the loft of our building. It wasn't so much should we look after her, but how could we do it. We knew the risk was there. But in wartime, anything you can do against the enemy, you just do. She would have been shot for certain. The danger to us was mentioned. If we were caught, we'd be in trouble. Perhaps we were over-confident. We thought, "We're British, we're protected by the Red Cross." '

Tommy Noble, a Scottish prisoner, put it more succinctly: 'She was a very nice wee thing and she'd been treated badly, like us. They were cruel pigs. We wanted to get them.'

When Sara, still very wary, reached the men's quarters, she found all ten living in a single room that was locked at night. It was in a stable block, half a mile from the nearest farm. The police kept horses there. Above was a hay loft. The prisoners hid Sara in a hole in the hay, next to a warm chimney coming up from their room. But first they gave her food:

'I gorged myself on soup and bread. It was milk and soup, a thin soup. I was bringing it up. One of them brought paraffin to clean the lice from my hair. They bathed me. I had sores on my legs. Bert Hamling was the medic. He brought some red ointment. They watched over me.'

Alan Edwards and George Hammond remembered her as all skin and bones. 'There were bruises on her arms, lice in her hair, slight frostbite on her feet. She had abrasions here and there. Her thighs were so thin you could ring them with your hands. She must have been half the weight of a normal sixteen year old, about five stones.' The men gave her solid food, meat from their rations. At first, she vomited it up, but gradually they noticed an improvement. The POWs would take food off their plates and smuggle it home to her. They kept a small stock of tea and sugar, and once a week each man received a Red Cross food parcel. They talked to her in their halting German. 'You had to understand the bloody guards,' one of them told me when I asked how they had learned it. 'If you didn't understand, they'd make you understand with the butt of a rifle.'

Edwards, the most resourceful of the ten Britons, stole clothes for Sara, a coat, a sweater, shoes and stockings. 'I already looked presentable,' she smiled in retrospect. After ten days they brought her down from the loft, though one of them always kept watch. After every visit, they eased her back through the trapdoor. They showed her a cupboard in their room and said that if the police took the hay out of the loft, they would hide her there behind a false wall. Despite the perpetual risk of discovery, it was an almost cosy interlude. The POWs saved Sara from the depredations of the SS guards and their ethnic German collaborators. They began the slow process of rebuilding her health and strength. And they convinced her that decency and courage were not entirely extinguished in a Europe laid waste by six years of war and genocide. 'I was so taken by how kind the British POWs were,' she reflected. 'It was the first kindness I had seen. They showed me there were still human beings. Somebody was going to take care of me, and I was ready for it.'

However, it was an interlude which could not last. After three weeks, Edwards broke the news that the POWs were being evacuated. Their German captors were joining the westward retreat. Edwards had arranged for a Polish workmate to come and pick Sara up. She passed a lonely, fearful night in the barn after her saviours had left. 'I waited for the fellow to come,' she said. 'I cried to myself. I felt very, very alone. I felt as I did in the trough. I wished myself dead.' The Pole never came, so Sara decided to leave. Around dawn, she went out. On the road, she passed a man who looked after the horses. She was sure he knew that she had been hiding above the stables, but he walked on to his work. The police stopped her, but let her go. Somehow Sara reached the farm where she had first met Stan Wells while hiding in the cowshed. 'I don't know how I found it,' she said. 'I felt there was some divine person taking care of me.' At the farm, she met the Russian girl who had refused to help her. She did not recognize the rehabilitated Sara and agreed this time to take her back to the labour camp. But Sara decided to take her chance outside. Her luck, divine or random, held – just. The Thousand-Year Reich was receding and the ethnic German villagers were more interested now in saving their skins:

'I got a job with a farmer called Heinrich Binder. He gave me a potato cellar to sort out. He said, "I think you're Jewish." I replied, "Yes, you're right." He was the head SS man in the village. He said, "Any other day I would kill you, but you're going to be my passport to life." I wrote him a postcard in Yiddish saying that he had saved me. He was hoping to make it west to Cologne, where he had relatives.'

The Binders fled before the Russians marched in, but the Jewish waif was waiting for them. It took her two more adventurous months to reach Bialystok, a textile city which had a Jewish community of almost 40,000 before the war. The Russians imprisoned her briefly on suspicion of spying. In Bialystok, she learned that her mother and sister, Hannah, had not survived the death march. She therefore added the name Hannah to her own in her sister's memory. In 1947, Hannah Sara emigrated to New York, where she had relatives. She studied nursing and later married William Rigler, now a justice of the New York state supreme court. She directs food distribution to the old and the homeless for the New York City Board of Education and chairs the Center for Holocaust Studies in Brooklyn.

Sara never forgot the British prisoners who restored her faith in humanity. The only full name she could remember was that of Alan Edwards. At one stage she persuaded a friend in England to ring everyone of that name in the telephone book. In 1964, with the help of the British War Office, she traced Edwards, who was running a car hire fleet in the Lancashire seaside resort of Morecambe. Eight years later she went to London and was reunited with all ten: Stanley Wells, Thomas Noble, George Hammond, Roger Letchford, Alan Edwards, William Keable, Bert Hambling, William Scruton, John Buckley and William Fisher. A second reunion followed in 1988, when BBC television told the story of these 'unsung heroes'.

In March 1989, Yad Vashem honoured them in Jerusalem. By then four of the ten had died and a fifth was too sick to make the journey. The five old soldiers, proud in their regimental blazers and campaign medals, planted a carob tree in the Avenue of the Righteous. 'We were two months on the march after we left her,' Alan Edwards recalled. 'We went to Danzig, where we were put into a party of 400, still in German hands. We were released on 9

May by the Americans. We often wondered what had happened to her. We hoped she'd come through.'

4

The Church Defiant

Erik Myrgren had not intended to stay in Berlin for more than two days. The thirty-year-old pastor was on his way home. His ministry to Swedish sailors in the Baltic city of Stettin had petered out, and the Allies had bombed his church in Krautmarkt. Although it was obvious by now that the war was lost, the Gestapo had become more and more menacing. Above all, Swedish ships were no longer calling. 'I was not needed any more,' he reported with ill-concealed relief. Myrgren was booked to fly on to neutral Stockholm in order to celebrate Christmas with his wife and small daughter. But November 1944 was no time for cosy domestic planning. Instead, the young pastor spent the last half year of hostilities outwitting the Nazi extermination machine in the heart of Hitler's capital. By fate or malicious design, Myrgren found himself the acting head of the Swedish church in Berlin, the last hope of dozens of hunted Jews who had somehow eluded five years of searches and betrayals, deportations and killings. When war broke out, the Jewish population of Berlin was estimated at 75,500. By the time the Nazis surrendered, there were 4,700 Jews married to Aryans in the city and 1,400 other Jews who had survived in hiding.

Myrgren was recruited overnight to the ranks of Christian clergy, Catholic, Protestant and Orthodox, who dedicated themselves to the witness of rescue – a Greek archbishop, an Italian monk, a Hungarian pastor, a Belgian abbé, a Polish mother superior who trained young partisans to throw grenades. There were others, among their colleagues and their superiors, who behaved more circumspectly, but for these men and women of God sheltering Jews became a vocation. They were defying the Devil. They personified a creed beyond private or political calculation, the creed of 'Love thy neighbour', the compassion of the Good Samaritan.

Pastor Myrgren was greeted at the Berlin railway station by the vicar of the Swedish church, Erik Perwe. The younger man, ordained only two years earlier, was still more student than preacher, dark-haired and heavy-featured with an enthusiasm for nature and folk songs. Perwe told him that he planned to fly to Sweden for two weeks at the end of November and asked Myrgren to stand in for him. So long as he could still get home for Christmas, Myrgren had no objection. He knew nothing of Perwe's undercover efforts to get the Jews out of Germany. He found out soon enough.

'Officially [Myrgren wrote forty years later] Perwe was leaving in order to collect food and clothes for needy Swedes in Berlin. In reality, however, he was planning a mass evacuation of Jews, who had managed to escape the Gestapo. During his time in Berlin, Perwe had succeeded in making contact with people in the highest leadership of the state, and there are those who say that he gained their silent agreement to what he was doing. There are also indications that he was sent on a secret mission from certain Nazi leaders willing to surrender to representatives of the Allied forces in Stockholm, and that he took important documents with him on the journey.

'I knew nothing of all this when I said goodbye to him on the morning of 29 November. He was in the very best of spirits. Some hours later there was a telephone call. The 'plane carrying Perwe and the other passengers had disappeared into the sea. Where and how nobody knew. The details were very sketchy. Rumours soon spread that the accident had been arranged, that the Gestapo had traced the traitors and ordered the 'plane to be shot down. Whether the rumours were true or not I am unable to judge.'

What Myrgren was able to judge was that Perwe's death put him on the spot. He would have to take over, yet he was neither trained for the task, nor briefed on its scope. He confessed to panic, but he was not left long in ignorance:

'The news of Perwe's death spread rapidly. A stream of people came to the church to pay condolences. Many shed tears. There were members of the congregation and of the Swedish Legation. There were German friends, high officials and common people. In the night his special friends came, Jews whom he had hidden and promised further help, people to whom he had been the border between life and death. I can still hear their cries of sorrow. Trembling old people, youngsters with despair in their eyes.'

Myrgren found a mentor in Erik Wesslen, a young lay worker at the church who had gone to Berlin to study landscape gardening. He was, Myrgren learned, the perfect fixer:

'He had a clear intellect, was full of ideas, brave and adventurous. He bought cars for a few kilos of coffee, and managed to get coal for heating and petrol for the vehicles. He got building material and workers when things needed to be repaired. And, last but not least, he bribed guards and policemen to let captured Jews disappear. It was a terrible, but necessary business. Buying people. Jews for coffee, alcohol, chocolate, money and jewels.'

Myrgren shared Wesslen's youthful exuberance – and his commitment. In his first post after ordination, he was assigned to assist a dean whose entire family turned out to be Swedish Nazis. Young Myrgren told him in front of others that he was a disgrace to the Swedish Church. The dean called him a Bolshevik and threw him out. When he was still a student in Uppsala, Myrgren befriended a young German whose father was a pacifist and had sent him to Sweden to evade military service. In 1941, the young man received his call-up papers. He went straight to the German Embassy, renounced his citizenship and asked Sweden for political asylum. Within days, he was summoned by the police and informed that asylum had been refused. The German begged Myrgren to help him. Myrgren sent him to his parents in the north, despite the severe penalties decreed for anyone hiding refugees. Then Myrgren lobbied Stockholm to grant his friend asylum. That, he said half a century later, was where it all began.

For the Church of Sweden, it had begun a decade earlier when Pastor Göte Hedenqvist had been sent to Vienna at the request of the Austrian Evangelical Church to help baptized Jews already threatened by pro-Nazi persecution. When hundreds of unconverted Jews begged him to assist them too, he decided that he could not distinguish between baptized and non-baptized. As a result of his efforts, 1,000 Jewish children and 2,000 adults are estimated to have been evacuated from Austria between 1935 and 1939. Erik Perwe went to Vienna to observe his work and returned home to lecture on the plight of Austrian Jews. His advocacy brought him to the attention of Archbishop Earling Eidem, who sent him to Berlin in 1939 to bring Jews out. The pastor in charge, Birger Forell, had been helping Jews ever since Hitler's takeover in 1933, but by 1941 he had received so many Nazi warnings that he could no longer continue. Perwe was his natural successor, as head of the church and as conspirator-in-chief. When his 'plane went down in the Baltic, Myrgren happened to be in the right place at the right time.

'Slowly, slowly [he wrote], I myself became part of the machinery which Perwe and Forell had built up so carefully. Its purpose was to help persecuted and bereaved people. Together with others in the church – Wesslen, Vide Ohmann, Meri Siöcroona, Birgitte Kruger, Wendela Rudbeck and little Jadja – I did what had to be done. People needed help, that was all. Help with food and clothing, a place to hide, transport to a secure place, some money, maybe medical care, or just some words of comfort and hope.'

Myrgren never forgot one particular Jew, Herbert Friedmann: 'He was fifty, but looked like seventy. He had once filled an important post. He was extremely thin and frightened. He was living like a shadow, afraid of being caught and transported away.' Perwe had promised to send Friedmann to Sweden and, when his hopes were dashed, he beseeched Perwe's successor to shelter him in the church, a villa set in its own grounds on the Landshausstrasse:

'I knew that Friedmann lived in a relatively secure place, so I answered, "We already have far too many people in the church. Be patient, maybe we will find something." Again, he begged to be allowed to stay. He could take no more. In order to calm him down, I promised to deal with the matter and asked him to come back a week later. The next day he was sitting in front of me again with the same request. I had so many urgent and difficult things to deal with, so I reminded him of the promise he already had. "In another week I may have a solution."

'The following day a certain "Dr Wiehle" called me and said, "I have a patient here. I cannot tell you his name, but he is in a serious condition and needs care. There is no hospital for him, but I have told him about you and the church. If you can, please take care of him for a few days." During the conversation I sensed something familiar, but I didn't say anything. "OK, let him come and we shall see what we can do."

'The patient came. It was Friedmann. I let him sit down, then I said in a friendly tone, "Dear Friedmann, I know that it was you who 'phoned. I have obviously not understood how difficult things are for you." Then I was interrupted. I was horrified to see him fall on his knees, crawling up against me and crying, "Let me stay! Let me stay!" It was so painful that I had to look away. I was so ashamed. But within me there grew a burning hatred against this system which so deeply humiliated a people and crushed its dignity that an old man found it proper to beg for his life at a young lad's feet. It was terrible, but it was good for me. It strengthened my inner readiness. It had been there before. Now it had found maturity and strength. I was afraid, but what had I to fear? Death was always close. The bombs were falling day and night. To take an additional risk meant so little. But for some people it was a matter of survival.'

Myrgren let Friedmann stay, putting him in the care of Martin and Margot Weissenberg, a Jewish couple who had lived in the church since March 1943, when they were bombed out of the old-age home where they had been hiding. Martin, in his sixties, and Margot, twenty years younger, were among the very few Jews who stayed in the church long-term. They became part of Myrgren's team. The pastor preferred to find havens for the Jews, often with brave German anti-Nazis, but forty or fifty refugees often spent the night under his roof. They were not all Jews. There were Swedes who had been living in Germany and were now making their way home as the Allied armies closed in. There were members of Myrgren's congregation whose homes had been bombed. And, after dark, came the Jews and forced labourers who had managed to escape, as well as army deserters on the run. The Swedish Legation had warned successive pastors that it could give them no diplomatic umbrella, but the church turned away no one in need.

Not all of the callers, Myrgren soon learned, were what they claimed. A tall, blond man came to the church one day and asked for help. He said that he was an Orthodox Jew. The pastor, who had learned some Hebrew at the seminary, asked him to recite a blessing. The man could not manage even the opening words, 'Baruch Atah Adonai', 'Blessed Art Thou, O Lord'. Another man, a bona-fide Jew, talked his way through and was smuggled by bus to Sweden in March 1945 under a deal between the SS chief, Heinrich Himmler, and the Swedish diplomat, Count Folke Bernadotte, for repatriating Swedish émigrés. 'I got to know years later that this man was an informer,' Myrgren confided. 'It pains me to this day.'

The Swedish pastors could not have achieved what they did without the co-operation of German anti-Nazis, who passed information and took fugitives into their homes. Two unlikely, but crucial, allies were Hoffman, the chief of the police station opposite the church, and one of his guards, Matteck. They warned the pastors when the Gestapo was approaching, transmitted messages and kept spies at bay. Matteck was a typical earthy Berliner, always making skittish jokes about 'die grossen da oben' ('the big guys up there') and dismissing the clubfooted Goebbels's propaganda broadcasts as 'klumpfusschens marchen-stunden' ('clubfooted fairy-tale time'). Matteck kept an army deserter hidden in the basement of the police station.

It was Matteck who procured false passports for Martin and Margot Weissenberg, stamped with permission to leave, in the names of the Swedes Martin and Margot Berg. Myrgren and young Erik Wesslen drove them to Tempelhof airport for the flight to Stockholm. But even with the right papers, Myrgren knew, their departure was fraught with danger:

'Passport control at Tempelhof was like the eye of a needle. There were all kinds of policemen and Gestapo people examining the passports. The Weissenbergs' passports were written in the name of Berg, and the permission to leave was cleanly stamped, but nobody knew for sure whether the corresponding information was inscribed on the police checklist. The Swedish airline representative in Berlin was indispensable. He had access to the airport offices and knew the people working there.

'Early in the morning, the agent left before us and went to Tempelhof well supplied with bottles of good cognac. The Weissenbergs had not slept all night. The evening before we had thrown a little party for them in order to give them and us some courage. But when we left in the little church DKW car next morning everyone was silent. Only Margot sobbed now and then when she saw the destruction in the streets. They had not been outside the walls of the church for more than a year.

'The airline man met us at the airport. He had already checked things and thought all was well. But all four of us – the Weissenbergs, Wesslen and I – were too excited to take his word for it. He took the passports and left us. I can still see how the smoke from my cigarette spouted from my trembling hand. I smoked one, two, three . . . We tried to speak, but we couldn't. Our throats were dry. Our hearts were beating. Our necks and faces were as hot as a fever. Why didn't he come? Then, at last, he stood there, discreetly waving the passports at us. The plot had succeeded. We walked calmly towards him. Everything must look normal. It turned into a silent farewell, but one filled with joy. With tears in my eyes, I watched the 'plane disappear in the morning haze.'

Sometimes the pastor himself was able to help Jews to obtain false papers. After the registration office in a district of Berlin had been bombed, the German authorities advertised asking people to bring whatever identification they had to receive new documents. A Jewish woman asked Myrgren if he could give her the name of a Swedish woman born in Berlin at about the same time as herself, but who had gone back to Sweden. The pastor found a suitable name in the church records and gave the Jewess a note certifying that she was this woman. Years later the Jewess wrote to him from the United States thanking him for saving her life.

But not all Myrgren's charges and allies scraped home. 'Many times', he wrote, 'it was a matter of disappointment and fright during this time of agony. For many the help came too late. Others were caught on the very doorstep to freedom.' Matteck, the earthy Berlin policeman, fell on 1 May 1945, the last day of the Red Army siege of the capital. 'He who had helped so many and who had watched over the church as if it were his own property, he was killed by a grenade as he was on his way to see our wards in the basement of the church. I was sitting in the bunker of the legation two kilometres away. The news was brought to us by a Jew, who ignored the heavy firing because of Matteck.'

Three days later, Russian soldiers set fire to the Swedish church. Myrgren and his team took sanctuary in the legation until they were evacuated to Sweden by way of the Soviet Union. The pastor settled back into the peace of an obscure rural parish, with one more excursion into a wider, more troubled world, supervising an exchange of prisoners in Korea. 'Exciting,' he told a Swedish reporter, 'but you couldn't compare it with Berlin. In Korea we were more or less spectators.' The reporter, Lars-John Lindberg of the *Sydsvenska Dagbladet*, sensed a certain nostalgia, not for war and the horror of war, but 'maybe for adventure and the chance to take a risk'.

· • ·

The Germans were hunting the Jewish children in his care. The Red Army was at the gates of Budapest. But Pastor Gabor Sztehlo, of the Hungarian Evangelical Church, was not going to be denied his Christmas party. In December 1944, there were about thirty-five children and young people in his hostel, a spacious hilltop villa belonging to a wealthy manufacturer. More than half of them were Jews, living under false names and identity cards, but that didn't stop them from gathering around the Christmas tree, singing carols and even performing in a Nativity play. The pastor, a tall, broad-shouldered man, elegantly dressed as always in a suit and tie, distributed packets of sweets. The Soviet artillery bombardment came as no surprise. The older children and the deaconesses who looked after them had reinforced the room with mattresses on the inside and wooden beds on the outside. But the first shells broke up the party. Everybody rushed for the shelter. 'When we came back,' one of the young Jews, David Peleg, remembered, 'the mattresses had been blown outside and the beds inside. Only the Christmas tree was not damaged. Sztehlo made a little speech saying everything had been bombed, but the Christmas tree had survived. Perhaps, he said, it was a sign from God.'

The hilltop hostel was one of thirty havens the Lutheran pastor had set up since the Germans had occupied Hungary in March 1944. They were Christian institutions. Prayers were the order of the day, and grace was said before meals. Although most of the boys and girls were Jewish, Jesus was invited to bless the bread, but survivors insist that the pastor and his staff never attempted to

Above: Pastor André Bettex, who shielded Jews in Le Chambon-sur-Lignon

Left: Sempo Sugihara, the Japanese Consul in Kovno

ristides de Sousa Mendes, the Portuguese Consul-General in Bordeaux, with his wife Angelina

Left: Charles Coward, the 'Count of Auschwitz', who saved Jews from the gas chambers by trading dead Jews for live ones. Here he is seen arriving at Frankfurt airport on his way to testify a slave labour suit against I. G. Farben

Below: Sara Rigler (Matuson) with fiv of the British prisoners of war who saved her life: (left to right) George Hammond, Alan Edwards, Tommy Noble, Roger Letchford and Stan We Jerusalem, 1989

Right: The false identity papers of Gabor Berger (Shmuel Ben-Dov) supplied by Pastor Gabor Sztehlo

Below: Archbishop Damaskinos with King George of the Hellenes on his return from exile

Above: Anna Borkowska receiving the Medal of the Righteous from the Israeli poet and former ghetto fighter, Abba Kovner, in Warsaw, 1984

Left: Zayneba Hardaga (centre), flanked by her sister, Arifagic Nada, planting a sapling in Jerusalem, June 1985. On the right is Yosef Kabilio.

Below: Selahattin Ulkumen, the Turkish Consul in Rhodes, at Yad Vashem, Jerusalem June 1990

ght: The Albanian Muslims
sel and Fatima Veseli (seated
tre) with the Jewish families
y sheltered in 1944. Moshe
d Gabriella Mandil are in the
ck row left; Gavra and Rina
andil are in front of their
rents. This photo was taken
tside the village house where
y were hidden.

ow: Liberation Day, Tirana,
vember 1944. Refik Veseli
cond from left) is in partisan
iform. The photographer
shad is third from left. Moshe
andil is second from right and
son Gavra is in the front
rsing a bottle of Chianti.

Above: Henryk Grabowski (second right) with Jewish resistance veterans in 1985. Chaika Grossman is in the centre, with Abba Kovner on the left.

Above: Yvonne Nevejean, the saviour of many Belgian Jewish children, in Brussels, 1969

Left: The German sergeant-major, Hugo Armann, planting a tree in the Avenue of the Righteous at Yad Vashem in 1986

Above: The rubber stamp made by Moshe Bejski for Oskar Schindler in 1945

Right: A railway document for Jews transported from Golleschau, a branch of Auschwitz. Oskar Schindler has crossed out various stations and written in 'Zwittau', the town nearest his factory, so that he could save their lives.

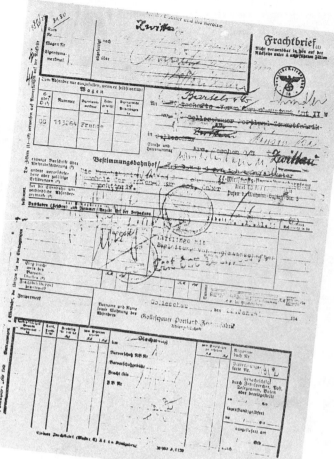

ow: Oskar Schindler in Cracow, 1942. His factory is in the kground.

Left: Max Schmeling being proclaimed the winner after his sensational victory over Joe Louis in 1936

Above: Maria von Maltzan, who sheltered Jews in her home in Berlin

Left: 'All that remained', a sculpture b Elsa Pollak in the museum at Yad Vashem, inspired by a display of victim shoes at Auschwitz

convert them. The prayers were silent, and each prayed in his own way. The Jews were never taught the New Testament. Before the occupation, Sztehlo had supervised religious education for working-class pupils in a network of 'people's academies', but once the Germans came in the Bishop of Budapest, Sandor Raffay, assigned him to rescue Jewish children.

With the help of the International Red Cross – and the flexible goodwill of its local delegate, Friedrich Born, whose exploits are described on pages 59–61 – he saved 905 Jewish children and 635 adults in the turbulent last year of the war. The pastor was aware that the penalty for hiding Jews was death. Red Cross protection had its limits. After the Arrow Cross Party seized power under the Germans in April 1944, for instance, a gang of these Hungarian Fascists raided a hospital, dragged out Jews sheltering there, and shot them along with all the doctors and nurses in the hospital yard. But for Sztehlo rescue was a test of faith. 'Christianity', he wrote in bold type in his memoirs, 'is not the world of dogmas, but of love. Of a living, lively and active love.'

Tibor Berger, a seventeen-year-old religious Jew, was one of the beneficiaries of this Christianity in action. In November 1944, he was drafted to labour on public works sites outside Budapest. After three weeks, he ran away and returned to the capital. He sought protection at a home Sztehlo ran for Christian refugees, youngsters who had escaped from areas of Hungary already under Soviet occupation. Tibor had papers identifying him as a Christian refugee, but he admitted to the pastor that he was Jewish. Sztehlo took him in none the less. Tibor soon realized that all of his 150 fellow boarders, as well as the nurses and teachers, were Jews.

Within a few days, however, the home was raided by the Arrow Cross. The Fascists rounded up all the able-bodied Jews and took them to a ghetto, where all the Budapest Jews were being concentrated. When the Arrow Cross began combing the ghetto for young people to work as slave labour in the Reich, Tibor ran away again. Finding that his first Christian hostel had been evacuated, he tried a second in an Evangelical boarding-school:

'After much danger, hungry and exhausted, I arrived at the institution, but I was told I must obtain a special entrance pass from the director. The institution had two offices, one in Pest, the other in Buda. The man in charge of the Buda office was Pastor Sztehlo, but I decided not to put my life in further danger by going there. To get to Buda I would have had to cross heavily guarded bridges, which had been mined. Not to mention the fact that the entire Gestapo lived near Sztehlo's home, with a heavy guard in front of each house.

'I decided to chance my luck at the Pest office, whose director was another Evangelical minister. I showed him papers which said I was a Christian named Kocsis Geza, a refugee from Mezokovesd. After a thorough check he invited me into a separate room, where he told me that he thought my papers were false and that I was a Jew. He couldn't accept me into his Evangelical institution. In deep despair, I decided after all to endanger my life – whatever would be, would be. I had to get to Sztehlo, the only man I could pin my hopes on. I crossed to Buda by train. The police were checking papers at the Buda side, but luckily nobody asked me for mine. At every corner near Sztehlo's house there were armed guards, but again I was lucky. Nobody challenged me. Sztehlo himself answered the door. He remembered me and gave me a warm welcome. He issued me with an entry permit to the children's home and changed the age on my papers from seventeen to sixteen so that I would not be drafted for the army. The Hungarians were calling up Christian boys at seventeen.'

Tibor discovered that his mother was living in a safe-house run by the Swiss embassy on one side of the city, while his sister, disguised as a Christian, was on the other. It was impossible for them to communicate with each other. When Tibor tried to visit them, he was told that identity papers were being checked throughout the city. Once again, he turned to the good pastor. Sztehlo got him a job as a Red Cross messenger, delivering potatoes and other vegetables to the hostels. With the help of Red Cross papers, he was able to visit his mother and sister, and sometimes to take them food.

In the last week of December, between Christmas and New Year, orders were given to search Tibor's hostel. The two directors, who shared responsibility for ensuring that there were no Jews hiding on the premises, arrived from Buda and Pest respectively. They came before the Germans to check that everything was in order. The young fugitive was in danger again:

'The Pest director recognized me and of course wanted to throw me out then and there. He was very surprised that I had reached the institution after all. Then Sztehlo intervened on my behalf and explained something to him in Latin, something he evidently didn't want me to understand, and persuaded him to let me stay.'

David Peleg, now a member of Kibbutz Daliah, was three years younger than Tibor. He was recommended to the hostel, where Sztehlo sang his carols around the Christmas tree, by a church worker who was a family friend. But after about two weeks, on 3 January, orders were given to evacuate the villa, which commanded a strategic hilltop. The Germans took them away to Sztehlo's house, where the pastor lived with his wife, son, aged about seven, and daughter, aged about four:

'The Germans didn't know we were Jews. One soldier carried a four-year-old Jewish boy on his shoulders. Sztehlo's wife, Ilona, knew we were Jews, but the family hid us, thirty-five children, in their home. For three weeks they endangered their lives trying to get food and water for us. They put us in a coal cellar, which was divided up by boxes. My box was so small that I didn't have enough room for my feet.'

Another of the boys in the cellar, Gabor Vermes, now a college professor in New Jersey, remembered the Jewish children singing songs in German to Wehrmacht officers who visited the basement. The local commander, a major, became friendly with the Sztehlos. He was sad and resigned, a soldier who understood the futility of the war.

'He once told Sztehlo that he knew who these children were [Vermes wrote], but he hated any form of racism and wished Pastor Sztehlo and all of us well. Before being transferred, he warned Sztehlo about an SS lieutenant whose main preoccupation was hunting down and killing Jews. I remember this lieutenant, with his black death's head armband, listening to our singing. Luckily, the lack of electricity meant that we did our activities by the dim light of kerosene lamps, so that he could not see us well. Perhaps the fact that he had drunk several glasses of wine before he came to the basement had dampened his hunting instincts. In any case, we remained undetected.

'Four weeks passed, our food was down to starvation levels, water was scarce and, soon, we were covered by fleas. On 29 January, early in the morning, something blew up in the basement.

It was a hand-grenade that had been thrown down by a Russian soldier. Luckily, no one was hurt. A Communist writer, who had been hiding with us and who spoke fluent Russian, shouted out, "There are no Germans here, only children and civilians." One of our German regulars, a certain Lieutenant Konig, and his men had put up such a stiff fight that the Russians were certain that our building was a German stronghold. Even after occupying it, they thought the Germans might have moved down into the basement. The Russians, rather than risking their lives in ferreting out the Germans, had planned to set the whole house on fire. Seconds before they were about to pull the trigger of the flamethrower, the writer yelled up in Russian, and we were liberated rather than burned to death.'

The liberation brought fresh tests for Pastor Sztehlo. It was widely feared that the Soviet Communists would kill the children of the Hungarian aristocracy. Sztehlo gathered these children along with other waifs and strays of all classes into a kind of boys' town, which he called Gaudiopolis, the joyous city. Its declared aim was 'to educate young people in the spirit of Christ, abolish social barriers, and transform these young people into independent, conscientious and well-educated citizens of Hungary'. Before emigrating to Israel, David Peleg found himself living and studying alongside the sons of barons and counts. 'He took us from villa to bigger villa, then to a kind of palace, three big houses in a park. I remember boys from the Bethlem, Apor and Gara families, noble families of Hungary who had provided prime ministers and cardinals.' Not surprisingly, Sztehlo fell foul of the new Communist Government, which wanted to nationalize Gaudiopolis and give the children a secular education.

The boys' town was taken over by the state in January 1950. Pastor Sztehlo served for the next decade as head of a Lutheran children's home, then emigrated to Switzerland in 1961 with the blessing and relief of the Communist regime. He was honoured by Israel in 1972 and died two years later. Tibor Berger settled in Haifa, adopted the Hebrew name Shmuel Ben-Dov and opened a jewellery factory. He visited the pastor in Switzerland in 1964 and presented him with a silver-bound Bible from the Holy Land, in which he had inscribed: 'God protected me, through your hand.'

• • •

It is said that when the Nazi occupation authorities demanded the resignation of Archbishop Papandreou Damaskinos for opposing the extermination of Greek Jews, the head of the Orthodox Church replied, 'The priests of the Orthodox Church never resign. They stay in the place where God put them, even if they are hanged for it!'

On both moral and national grounds, Damaskinos took the lead in resisting the deportations, which began in Salonica in the spring of 1943. The Archbishop drafted and published a letter to the puppet Prime Minister, Constantinos Logothetopoulos, on 23 March denouncing the discriminatory treatment of Greece's 77,000 Jews, most of them Sephardim expelled from Spain in 1492. The letter, co-signed by the leaders of twenty-eight national business, professional and cultural organizations, insisted that 'all Greek citizens must enjoy the same treatment from the occupation authorities, regardless of race and religion'. Greek Jews, it added, had proved their loyalty to the Hellenic idea: 'They have made sacrifices as a community for the Greek homeland and have fought on the front lines in the wars of the Greek nation for its historic rights . . . Our holy religion does not recognize any distinction of superiority or inferiority based on race or religion.'

The letter ended with a warning that 'a day will come when the people will judge the deeds of this difficult time, even those that are done against our will and are outside our powers to control'. It had little immediate effect. Salonica, the home of 56,000 Jews, had been under German occupation since April 1941. Another leading churchman, Metropolitan Genadios, had intervened in January 1943, when the Nazis began to corral Jews into a ghetto. At the request of the Salonica lawyers' association, he offered church assistance in exiling the Jews to a remote Greek island instead of shipping them to the death camps. This appeal fell on deaf ears. Almost the entire Jewish population of the northern port city was sent to the concentration camps. About 52,000 died in Auschwitz alone. A few hundred escaped to Athens.

However, Archbishop Damaskinos had established a pattern of resistance. If the Jews of Salonica could not be saved, the Jews of Athens could. The capital was occupied by Italy until Mussolini's surrender in September 1943. The 3,000 Athenian Jews had enjoyed a period of relative security, but as soon as the Germans took control they too were marked for the Final Solution. Damaskinos summoned the director-general of the Athens municipality, Panos Haldezos, and told him, 'I have made my Cross, have spoken with God, and decided to save as many Jewish souls as I can.' Even if it meant endangering himself, he would baptize the Jews and Haldezos would register them as Christian Greeks. With the ready co-operation of the local police chief, Anghelos Evert, they shielded 560 Jews by this device. The Archbishop also ordered the clergy throughout Greece to help Jews and to open the monasteries to them. He arranged fictitious Jewish–Christian marriages and extended church protection to other Jews who really had married Christians.

The Archbishop's order bore fruit in Chalcis, on the Euboea peninsula north of Athens, and on the Ionian island of Zakynthos. Yitzchak Kerem, an historian of Greek Jewry, records that Metropolitan Gregorios of Chalcis protected the ancient Jewish community's Torah scrolls, complete with their silver ornamentation, until the liberation. Between 1,500 and 2,000 Jewish fugitives from Athens were hidden in nearby monasteries before escaping by fishing boat to neutral Turkey, where they boarded trains to Syria and Palestine. On Zakynthos, the Nazi governor, Alfred Lit, ordered the mayor, Lukas Karrer, to bring him a list of the island's 275 Jews. If he did not deliver the next day, Lit warned him, his life would be at stake. The mayor consulted Bishop Chrysostomos, who told him to burn the list. The clergyman arranged to bribe Lit with a diamond ring to forget about it. When a new German governor ordered Karrer to assemble all the Jews within twenty-four hours or face execution, the mayor alerted the Jews and urged them to flee to outlying villages and take refuge with Christian families. He then set sail for a neighbouring island, where he stayed in hiding until Zakynthos was liberated in September 1944. 'The Germans', Kerem wrote, 'retreated on the same three boats that were destined to deport the local Jewish community, but which were never utilized for that purpose.'

Most of the 10,000 Jews who survived the war in Greece owed their lives to the Athenian police. Inspired by Archbishop Damaskinos, Anghelos Evert's force not only issued false, though authentic, identification papers free of charge, but also went looking for Jews to receive them. Once they had these cards, the

Jews could travel freely and find new addresses. The papers carried conviction. Evert provided an Athenian couple, Mr and Mrs Haim Cohen, with papers identifying them as Pavlos and Marika Panopoulos.

'With the false papers [Cohen recalled] we lived anonymously in the Pangrati quarter of Athens from November 1943 until the liberation. These papers saved our lives because at midnight on 23 November Gestapo agents searched our home. They demanded our identity cards. With the help of God, they were convinced that they were authentic and they left without discovering our identities.'

Another Jewish recipient of the Evert cards was Sam Modiano, the former editor of a Salonica newspaper who served after the war as Reuters bureau chief in Athens.

'Mr Evert gave us identity cards with his official signature and with the official seal of the police department [Modiano reported]. They bore Greek names which indicated that we were of the Orthodox Greek faith. Thanks to these documents, we had no trouble living in the suburb of Athens where we were housed by friends until the liberation in October 1944. My son Elie was then twenty years old and used his false identity to leave secretly for the Middle East, where he enlisted in the Royal Greek Air Force.

'Mr Evert collaborated with Archbishop Damaskinos in the salvation of young Jewish girls whom they helped to find refuge with Christian families until the end of the war. Through his courageous deeds, the chief of police is acknowledged by all the Jews whom he helped one way or the other, even if just with good advice. He did so at the risk of his life, since he was constantly menaced by the possibility that one of his subordinates would betray him to Gestapo agents, Greek as well as German.'

Modiano brought 400 Salonica Jews to Athens with false passports issued by the Italian Consul-General, Giuseppe Castruccio. With the help of Christian friends, he housed them in two schools. When the Germans took over the capital in September 1943, they ordered the Chief Rabbi, Elia Barzilai, to bring them the names of the ten richest Jews in the city; to tell them where the Jewish community kept its funds; to reveal who was hiding the Salonica 'Italians'; and to give them Sam Modiano's address. Barzilai consulted his congregation and sent a warning to Modiano, who turned to Evert for advice:

'Mr Evert recommended that I move house immediately and that I go to the schools where the Jewish refugees were being sheltered and tell them to scatter themselves throughout the different quarters of the capital. Finally, Mr Evert advised me not to worry about Rabbi Barzilai. In fact, when the Germans began searching for the Chief Rabbi, they could not find him at his home or at the synagogue. Mr Evert had alerted members of the Greek resistance movement to the dangers facing the Jews if the Chief Rabbi had to meet again with the Nazis. At dawn a jeep stopped in front of the Chief Rabbi's residence and swept him and his family off to the mountains in eastern Greece which were under resistance control.'

• • •

For three years, from 1941 to 1944, Father Joseph André seldom slept a whole night in his bed. Even when he was resting, he stayed fully clothed and ready to receive any Jew seeking shelter. You did not need to knock on the door of his house near the church of St Jean Baptiste in Namur, thirty miles south-east of Brussels. It was always open. In co-operation with the Belgian resistance and Jewish defence organizations, he placed hundreds of children and adults with Christian families. But for Father (later Abbé) André that was only a beginning. He procured false identity papers and ration coupons for his charges. He made sure that they were being well looked after. He was their social worker and their education officer. At the slightest hint of danger, he moved them to new homes – in Namur and elsewhere. Until he found them a haven, he often kept children in his own house, with a hideout nearby in case the Gestapo came looking unannounced. When he himself had to evade the Germans, he continued his operations from hiding.

Arieh Vishnia, a member of the Jewish underground, sent dozens of refugees to the Catholic priest. 'No one turned to him for help without receiving an appropriate arrangement,' Vishnia testified. 'More than that, he followed up on every Jew for whom he found a hiding-place. And if it turned out that the place was not suitable or the treatment there not good, he would immediately move the Jew to another hiding-place.'

Rachel Segal's experience was one among many. She was a Jewish mother who was forced to flee the rooftop apartment, where her family had been hiding in Brussels, at the beginning of

1943. An acquaintance with a son in the resistance sent her to Father André:

'The father immediately gave me an address in Velbain sur l'Est. I arrived there and was given refuge by the Bernet family. I was hidden there for several months. I had to leave that place, so I went again to Father André for a new hiding-place. He directed me to a family in Namur itself. I could only stay there a few weeks, but during the whole time Father André came to visit me and checked on my safety. I had to change hiding-places several times in Namur, and each time it was Father André who found the new place and brought me to it. He was the only one who took care of me and who made sure I'd be in a safe place, knowing that no place could stay safe for very long. After Namur was bombed, Father André found me a hiding-place in Valso, where I stayed until the liberation. He also kept my son in hiding, making sure he could move from one safe place to another. His concern was so great that he made a special trip to Brussels and brought my small daughter, who was living with a family there, so that I could see her, and then took her back.'

Father André made sure that his Jewish wards did not forget their faith or their customs, even when they were placed in Catholic homes. It is said that all of them could sing 'Hatikvah', the Zionist anthem of hope and freedom. Gustave Collet, a young layman who worked with Father André, ferried groups of fearful children from town to town, reassuring them as best he could. Sometimes they had to hide for two or three days in a barn. To keep them occupied he gave lessons in Hebrew, which he had taught himself, and calmed them with Jewish songs and prayers.

The first Passover after the liberation, Father André entertained about 200 displaced Jews to a traditional seder feast in his house on the Rue de l'Ange (the Street of the Angel) in Namur. Sylvain Brachfeld, who was to write a book on the rescue of Jewish children, was the little boy who asked the customary four questions. Sylvain's mother, Ernestine, checked that everything was kosher. A man who had jumped from a train transporting him to the death camps led the service.

Father André remained in touch with some of his charges after the war and regularly attended an annual day of Bible study organized by Antwerp Jews. He was honoured by Yad Vashem in 1968.

• • •

What Father André did in Namur, Padre Rufino Nicacci did in Assisi, the birthplace of the gentle, ascetic St Francis. Assisi, in the foothills of the Apennines, had a population of about 5,000 in 1943. Not one of them was Jewish. Nor, so far as anyone knew, had any Jew lived there since the Middle Ages. The Umbrian town, with its medieval churches and monasteries, cathedral, castle and palaces, made its living from pilgrimage. Christians came to pray and to ponder. The clergy, some more worldly, some less, tended the shrines of St Francis and St Clare, the founders of the orders of Franciscans and Poor Clares. For nine months, from the start of the German occupation in September 1943 until the liberation in June 1944, Assisi became a sanctuary for people on the run from the Nazis – Jews, anti-Fascists, even two American airmen who baled out when their bomber was shot down.

The Bishop of Assisi, Monsignor Giuseppe Placido Nicolini, presided over a network of friars and nuns that hid up to 300 Jewish refugees, some in the closed inner cloister of a convent, and supplied forged papers for hundreds more. Father Nicacci, the brave, down-to-earth son of an Umbrian peasant family, was his principal troubleshooter, inventive, devious and persistent. The fact that he had never met a Jew before and knew nothing of their customs made no difference. The thirty-two-year-old Father Nicacci and his more phlegmatic partner, Don Aldo Brunacci, were doing the Lord's work. The Jews, they believed, had been entrusted to them by divine providence. 'With God's help,' Don Aldo wrote soon after the liberation, 'and through the intercession of St Francis, not one of them fell into the hands of their persecutors.'

It was a close call. Both Father Nicacci, father-guardian of San Damiano monastery, and Don Aldo Brunacci, canon of San Rufino cathedral, were arrested by the Gestapo and were threatened with execution or deportation to German death camps. During a night raid on the convents, Nicacci guided a group of Jews through a secret tunnel and into the hills with minutes to spare. As well as the Nazis, they had the Italian Fascist police, the OVRA, and potential informers to contend with.

Father Nicacci's first coup was to persuade a patriotic master printer, Luigi Brizi, to forge high-quality identity cards, complete with the crests of cities in southern Italy already under Allied control and thus beyond the reach of Gestapo investigators. Brizi and his son, Trento, worked night after night at the press. All of the Jews who sought shelter in Assisi were given new, Christian identities, generally with their original initials so that they were less likely to betray themselves under pressure. Those who spoke Italian and did not look particularly Semitic were thus able to mingle with other refugees who had come to the relative safety of the holy city, which also served as a hospital and rest centre for the Wehrmacht.

Emilio Viterbi, a chemistry professor who arrived from Padua with his wife and two daughters, was renamed Ernesto Varelli. His younger daughter, Mirjam, became Mirella. They were registered as natives of Lecce, in the far south-east, which had already fallen to the British. 'We spent hours learning about Lecce,' Mirjam told me. 'We learned the names of streets, hotels, public buildings. We learned about the history of our fictitious family and the place where my grandmother was supposed to have been born.'

The Viterbis, whose paternal ancestors had lived in Italy for nearly 2,000 years, lodged first in a small hotel, then in an apartment with the landlord living one floor below. The landlord and the hotel people knew that they were Jewish. On 1 December, three days after they had moved into the apartment, Armando Giacanella, who worked as a handyman at the hotel, came to them and said that he had heard on the radio that the Gestapo was looking for Jews. 'If you happen to know a Jew,' he smiled knowingly, 'you'd better warn him.' It sometimes seemed as if the whole town was in on the conspiracy. Viterbi's wife, Margherita, went one day to confront the mayor, Arnaldo Fortini, who was a Fascist, but also a leading Assisi lawyer and historian of the Franciscans. She wanted to broaden the range of their connections. 'There are four of us,' she told him. 'We are Jewish. Will you help us or will you betray us?' He answered without hesitation that he would help. More than once, when the Gestapo were hunting for Jews, the mayor kept his word and warned the Viterbis. In the final weeks of the occupation, the professor and his wife were visiting Don Aldo Brunacci when the Germans came to arrest him. Before being taken away, the priest asked permission to say goodbye to his mother. Instead, he came and signalled the Jewish couple to hide. Only the intercession of the Bishop prevented him from being transported to a concentration camp. Don Aldo was exiled to Rome until the liberation.

The network arranged for some children to attend local schools. 'We were particularly anxious that the Jewish boys and girls should not waste their time,' Don Aldo explained. 'Thanks to their false papers, several of them continued their studies in the public schools, while others were prepared privately and then presented themselves in the usual manner for the state examinations, at which I may say they did very well. After the liberation, of course, we corrected their names in the school records.' Professor Viterbi's daughters, Grazella and Mirjam, aged seventeen and ten respectively, went to church on Sundays with their heads veiled in decorous black lace. 'We sat at the side', Mirjam remembered, 'so as not to be conspicuous. We didn't like to cross ourselves, but sometimes when we felt we ought to we did it in the wrong order or with the cross incomplete.' Once, when there was an alarm, the Viterbi family requested the Bishop's protection. He volunteered to sleep in his study and let them use his bedroom.

Another refugee from Padua, Georgina Rietti, described how the Bishop drove her and her sister thirteen miles to Perugia to obtain ration cards from a municipal official who was a member of the network. 'We came back', she rejoiced, 'with a car full of pasta.' The genuine personal documents of the Jews were cached in the cellar of the Bishop's palace until the liberation, as were a Torah scroll and other religious objects they had brought with them. The Bishop himself cemented the entrance to the store-room by the light of a candle borne by Brunacci.

The indefatigable Father Nicacci hid other Jews, those who did not look or sound like Italian Christians, in monasteries and convents. The men were dressed in monks' habits and taught to pray and conduct themselves accordingly. Most newcomers were lodged in the guest-house of the Convent of San Quirico. Some were transferred to other havens once they acquired new identities. Others, especially foreign Jews, stayed under the sisters' roof. On the evening of 4 October 1943, the Gestapo conducted its first raids. By mobilizing the Bishop and with fictitious orders from the Pope, Father Nicacci persuaded an extremely reluctant abbess, Mother Giuseppina, to admit thirty Jews, men, women and children, to the secluded nuns' quarters behind a locked door and double grille. 'This was against the precepts of their order,' one of the refugees, Hannah Gelb, testified. 'The risks were tremendous because anyone hiding Jews faced the death penalty.' But once persuaded, there was no stopping Mother Giuseppina. With the Nazis at her door, she locked the Jews, the Bishop and Father Nicacci in the forbidden cloister, then single-handedly shamed the intruders into taking their guns and their questions off her sacred premises. 'I'm glad the Pontiff's orders came just in time,' Nicacci whispered to the Bishop. According to the padre's biographer, Alexander Ramati, the Bishop whispered back, 'The Pontiff, I am sure, would have given such orders if he were in my place.'

No attempt was made, in San Quirico or other monastic houses, to force Christianity on the hidden Jews. 'In the quiet of the Assisi convents,' wrote Don Aldo Brunacci, 'the Jews were completely free to join together for their devotions, and it often happened that while the nuns were at their prayers, close at hand, under the same roof, the Jews too were imploring the divine mercy and asking God for justice and peace.' Father Nicacci arranged for the Jews to man their own kosher kitchen. On 8 October 1943, at the end of the Yom Kippur fast, the sisters decorated the San Quirico refectory with flowers and staged a feast for their guests. Professor Viterbi and his family were among Jews outside the convent invited to join them. A few months later the priests faced a dilemma when an ailing Austrian Jewess, Clara Weiss, died in San Quirico. A *minyan* (quorum) of ten men recited *kadish*, the mourner's prayer, inside the convent. The coffin was then given a Christian burial in the cemetery of Assisi in the name of Clara Bianchi. When the sexton queried why the customary service in the cemetery chapel had been missed out, Don Aldo explained that they had prayed in the convent because of the bad weather. After the war, the cross over the grave was replaced by a Star of David and 'Bianchi' by 'Weiss'.

Father Nicacci's most perilous, and most audacious, mission was to deliver a group of fifteen Jews, disguised as Christian pilgrims, to a pair of mountain smugglers, who ferried them through a January snowstorm and across the river Sangro to the Allied lines. The trains were not running and trucks were searched at frequent checkpoints. The padre solved his transport problem by talking the local German commander, Colonel Valentin Müller, into providing a military vehicle, complete with driver and escort. The colonel, a genial army doctor and devout Catholic, had adopted Father Nicacci as his confessor. He had no enthusiasm for Hitler's racial policies, nor did he wish to terrorize Assisi. He took the padre at his word: the Jews were stranded Christmas pilgrims, their rabbi was their bishop. The colonel added a *laissez-passer* for good measure.

Three months later, four of the network's couriers, three young Jews and a partisan officer, were caught while delivering forged papers in Perugia. Their interrogators failed to break them. They stood by their cover stories and were eventually released, but one of them made a slip of the tongue that focused suspicion on the Assisi churchmen. The SS arrested Father Nicacci, who was thrown into solitary confinement without food. Before dawn each day he heard screaming prisoners being led out to face the firing squad, but he stubbornly refused to give the Nazis the information they wanted. On the third night the padre's turn came. He was taken from his cell and bundled into a truck with five other men. They were then driven into an enclosed yard at the old Perugia women's prison. The padre's five companions were lined up, blindfolded and shot. Captain Ernst von den Velde, the SS officer responsible for security in the region, had supervised the executions. Now he turned on Nicacci and gave him twenty-four hours to confess. The padre again refused and was locked back in his cell, where he fell asleep. When he awoke, he was given food and taken to meet a well-connected Perugia lawyer, who had pulled strings to secure his release. It had been the closest of calls.

Assisi was liberated by British tanks early on the morning of 17 June 1944, but not before the city too had evaded disaster by the skin of its collective teeth. Before withdrawing, the Wehrmacht began mining key buildings. Colonel Müller had no authority to stop the sappers, but one of Father Nicacci's undercover Jews, Paolo Jozsa, who had inveigled himself into a job with the Germans, arrived at the last minute with an order proclaiming Assisi an open city. The last Germans left quietly, and the Allies rode in without bloodshed. Among them was Alexander Ramati, a free Polish war correspondent. Thirty years later, Padre Nicacci confided to him that the open-city order had been a forgery.

. • .

The young resistance fighters, Socialist Zionists to a man and woman, called her '*Imma*', Hebrew for 'Mother'. Anna Borkowska, then about forty, was the Polish mother superior of a modest Dominican cloister in Kolonia Wilenska, three miles outside Vilna, a city from which the Nazis took and massacred 60,000 Lithuanian Jews in less than four months. She provided a refuge and a forum where ghetto fighters from Vilna (now Vilnius), Bialystok and Warsaw plotted insurrection by candlelight with the Lithuanian and Polish undergrounds. She was their mother and their comrade. Chaika Grossman, a future member of the Israeli parliament, remembered her as 'the kind of person you want to have as a friend'. She had a warm, straightforward personality and 'the face of a woman who loves human beings'. Abba Kovner, Hebrew poet and resistance leader, stayed there for weeks disguised as a novice (Grossman said that his long, poet's hair helped him to get away with it). 'He performed with exceptional responsibility all the tasks in our household he had taken upon himself,' Mother Borkowska recorded. 'He put on an apron, tied a kerchief around his head and went with us to work the fields. From afar he looked like a woman with a pale, ascetic face.'

Long afterwards, Kovner wrote that so many Jewish men and women found refuge behind the locked gate of the convent that they often outnumbered the seven or eight nuns:

'Despite the great danger and despite the growing objections of the local population and of her superiors, Anna Borkowska continued her rescue activities and widened her network of connections in order to provide safe hiding and safe papers for the Jews who came under her wing. It was not just a good place to hide. It was the stairway to rescue. And each and every one of the nuns there worked each and every day to ensure that rescue, and I don't even know their names. Between the walls of the cloister and with the mother superior's knowledge, secret meetings of Jewish ghetto leaders were held. Between the walls of this convent the first declaration of our uprising was composed in January 1942. When the fighters decided it was time to return to the ghetto, Anna

Borkowska aided them by keeping watch on the arms they had stored in the convent. One day this woman appeared, dressed in civilian clothes, at the gates of the ghetto, holding hand-grenades she had somehow obtained, the first hand-grenades of the ghetto underground. When she passed them to me her fingers were trembling, like a mother hen protecting her chicks under her wings. And she whispered, "God is with you, my dear one." To this day I can hear these words of parting.'

Another fighting poet, Avraham Sutzkever, wrote in his chronicle of the Vilna ghetto: 'The first four grenades received gratefully by the fighters were the gift of the mother superior, who instructed Abba Kovner in their proper use since the make was unfamiliar to him. She later supplied other weapons.'

It was an incongruous alliance. On one side the aspiring pioneers, all in their early twenties, dreaming of a revolutionary new society in a faraway land, yet determined, if necessary, 'to die the death of free people, with guns in our hands'. On the other a woman who had dedicated her life to prayer and contemplation. The Jews could not readily reconcile the fact that she was at once a science graduate of Cracow University and a holy sister. At their first encounter, she wrote, 'we looked at each other searchingly'. She tried to understand their ideas, but it was not easy. 'I had some very vague notions about Marxism, and since the discussion revolved around this we could not understand each other very well. It took me some time to come to terms with this completely new way of looking at things.'

Her favourite was Arieh Wilner, whom she gave the Aryan cover name of Jurek: 'Two different worlds met. Nevertheless, we found points of contact, or rather bridges, since each one of us wanted to be able to look into the other's soul. We had respect for each other's convictions. We exchanged our philosophies, not without some sort of influence on each other. In our discussions we tried to escape from the monstrous reality into the world of ideas.'

What she understood immediately was the young Jews' refusal to go quietly. Like them, she hated foreign domination. Like them, she was appalled by the 'Nazi terror', the slaughter in the killing fields of Ponary six miles from Vilna. But at first she urged them to save Jews, rather than to take up arms. 'She tried to convince us', Chaika Grossman recalled, 'that if the Germans really were planning to exterminate all Jews, our activities must concentrate on saving people, especially the activists from our movement, because the Jewish nation of the future would need such people. Later she understood that we could not be active only by saving our people.' Once persuaded, she set about finding contacts to supply weapons. Not all of the underground groups were eager to co-operate. Some were tainted with anti-Semitism; others doubted the Jews' patriotic commitment.

The Jewish fighters soon became 'my boys and girls'. When word came from Warsaw that the Jews must prepare to defend themselves, she detected a tragic obstinacy. 'I bade them farewell with a heavy heart. I knew what was in store for them.' When she visited them in Vilna, she abandoned her nun's habit. One snowbound night, she arrived on skis.

Many of her boys and girls sacrificed their lives. She grieved for them one by one: Arieh Wilner, who died in the battle for the Warsaw ghetto; and other less celebrated martyrs, remembered affectionately by their first names:

'Yisrael was a good-natured, quiet boy. He worked picking berries. He was the first to go to Warsaw. One day at dawn he set out with a rucksack. The road was dangerous, he had "non-Aryan" features. I worried about him, but I finally believed that he would make it. I wanted to make him believe it too. And he made it! But he suffered terrible misery in the Warsaw ghetto. He wrote me a most cordial note, which I shall never forget. He perished in Treblinka . . .

'And my girls. Tauba, who loved life so much. Gentle, pleasant, she nevertheless had the courage to throw a grenade under a German car and to die a heroic death. Sarenka, a delicate and loving mother, who bravely bore up under the death of her husband and separation from her child. She went to Warsaw and lost her life there. Wirka, liaison officer from the ghetto, who placed mines on the tracks, then came rushing over to us for a cup of tea.'

Anna Borkowska mourned too the non-combatants, women and children, who found temporary sanctuary in her cloister. 'Mrs K' was a grandmother who, trembling and in tears, arrived one October night, when 35,000 Jews perished in a single 'action'. The mother superior found her kind-hearted, industrious and devout:

'Sometimes I talked to her for a long time. She was trying to alleviate her sorrow by remembering the past, telling us about her sons. Sometimes she was torn by terrible doubts. Could God be good if he permitted such monstrosities to happen? She stayed with us until we all had to leave our little house. On a small sledge I brought little Sala, Mrs K's granddaughter. She was four years old and did not speak Polish. Her father ordered her not to open her mouth during the journey. She sat quietly and seriously while on the way, then later at home she wouldn't open her mouth either. But once, when there was a noise in the courtyard, the little one asked gravely, "Granny, must we go now to Ponary?" She perished in Ponary, with her grandmother.'

The church authorities dispersed the convent at Kolonia Wilenska in 1943 after the nuns fell under Gestapo suspicion, first in March then in September, when two were arrested. One of the nuns was sent to a forced labour camp. The mother superior was interrogated. After the liberation, Anna Borkowska gave up the veil. Abba Kovner, who traced her many years later living on a pension in Warsaw, believed that she could not forgive the closure.

In 1984, Yad Vashem sent Kovner to Warsaw to present her with the Medal of the Righteous. 'I don't know if God was with us,' he said, 'but it was clear to me that this woman's face accompanied us and was a source of inspiration. For all who wandered in that desert of animosity, she was with them at the time the angels mourned.'

5

The Benevolent Crescent

'Yosef, you are our brother, and Rivkah, you are our sister, and the children are our children. Everything we have is yours, this is your home.' In Sarajevo in April 1941, the Arabian Nights greeting meant more than the usual effusive eastern hospitality. In a gesture that made him one of the four Muslims decorated by Israel for saving Jews, Mustafa Hardaga, a merchant who owned property all over the city and dealt in Persian carpets, was offering a roof to his friend and tenant, Yosef Kabilio, after the German air force had bombed him out of his third-floor apartment. Mustafa shared the rambling house with his older brother, Izet. Their wives, Zayneba and Bahria, lived in separate women's quarters and veiled their faces with their pinafores when they saw Yosef. They had never before had a strange man to stay with them.

Soon after their Jewish guest moved in with his wife, son and daughter, the Wehrmacht entered the Yugoslav city, where the assassination of the Archduke Franz Ferdinand in 1914 had triggered the First World War. About a third of the population were Muslims, many of whom collaborated with the invaders. There was an upsurge of anti-Semitism. The Great Synagogue, which was in the same neighbourhood as the Hardaga home, was sacked by a mob. Priceless Torah scrolls, dating back to the expulsion of the Jews from Spain more than 400 years earlier, went up in flames. The Germans, aided by the local security police, began mass deportations of the city's 10,000 Jews, ninety per cent of them Sephardi, in September 1941. Yet Mustafa and Zayneba, who was twenty years his junior, kept faith with the Kabilios, even when the

Gestapo set up an interrogation centre opposite their house and posters went up throughout the city threatening death to anyone who hid Jews.

Yosef Kabilio watched the anti-Semitic riots from behind a curtain in the Hardaga mansion. 'These deeds', he testified, 'only strengthened the Hardagas' feelings of friendship towards us and their sympathy for what was happening to the Jews.' But Yosef was worried that their presence was endangering his hosts. He found a Serbian friend, who smuggled Rivkah and the children, disguised as his own family, to the relative safety of the Italian-controlled zone of Yugoslavia. However, Yosef, one of Sarajevo's leading manufacturers, was too well known to accompany them. He would have been recognized at the first checkpoint.

The occupying regime ordered the transfer of his factory, which produced high-quality plumbing materials, to his chief accountant, an ethnic-German collaborator named Eterle. When some of the workers sabotaged two machines to stop them falling into German hands, Eterle immediately accused Kabilio of complicity.

'I understood that he would try to have the regime arrest me [Yosef wrote]. I knew I had to find a hiding-place away from the Hardaga family, who lived so close to the factory. When darkness fell I made my way to the military hospital, where an old friend of mine, Captain Radovich, was in charge. I asked him to hide me. He decided that the best and only way was to disguise me as a sick prisoner.'

Kabilio stayed in the military hospital for two months, but one night the police came and arrested him. He was held with seventy other Jews in the local prison. Because of an exceptionally hard winter, the Germans were unable to transfer them, as planned, to the Jasenovac slave labour camp in northern Yugoslavia. Instead, they were taken out every morning to shovel snow off the streets. One day, as they were making their way back to their cells, chained together, Kabilio spotted a veiled woman, weeping as she stood and stared at the prisoners. He recognized her as Zayneba Hardaga. 'From that day,' he wrote, 'for the whole month that I was imprisoned, Zayneba and her sister-in-law brought enough food for me and a few other hungry mouths.'

A month was long enough, however. One night Kabilio and

another Jewish prisoner escaped. Kabilio, who was then forty-five, had kept in good shape: he was a keen sportsman, a skier and a mountain-climber. These skills served him well. He jumped from a third-floor window on to the roof of an abandoned house, then fled to the railway station and hid in an empty freight car. But an informer told the police and he was recaptured. The Gestapo sentenced him to death and sent him, along with eight other condemned men, to a place called Pale, about twenty miles from Sarajevo. Partisans had sabotaged water and sewage pipes, and the prisoners were set to work repairing them. 'Our jailers didn't bother themselves about food for us,' he recalled, 'so we lived on the grass and snails.' Once again, the Hardaga family intervened. One of their guards happened to know the Muslim merchant and casually mentioned Kabilio and the other prisoners. 'Two weeks later, when I had reached my lowest ebb because of the lack of food and the harsh labour, they managed to get food parcels to us. The courage of the Hardaga family touched all of us, and gave us strength to keep living in our imprisonment.'

Two months after their arrival in Pale, the guards received an order to execute the nine prisoners. Before it could be carried out, Captain Reinman, an officer in the Domobrany, the Yugoslav standing army, came during the night to their prison shack and said that he would leave the door open. The captain, Kabilio's son Benny speculated in 1990, might have been Jewish. The prisoners did not need to be told twice. They slipped out while it was still dark, each going his own way.

'Since I was familiar with the surrounding mountains [Yosef wrote], I decided to return to Sarajevo through the woods. Before dawn I was knocking on the door of the Hardaga family. After all the risks they had taken for me, bringing me food and so on, I knew I could depend on them. They were extremely happy to see me, laughing and crying at the same time. They told me that they were sending money to my family with every chance they could get. That was the first night in months that I was able to sleep well.'

The next morning Kabilio met Zayneba's father, Ahmed Sadik, who told him that he had hidden the Papo family, Jewish friends of the Kabilios, and had managed to get them to the Italian zone. Ahmed Sadik was later denounced for helping Jews and was killed in Jasenovac. In the Hardaga home, Kabilio ate well and began to recover. But at night he could hear the screams of Communist resistance fighters being tortured in the cellars of the Gestapo headquarters across the road.

'I began to notice things around me, notices plastered on walls warning the public against sheltering Jews or Communists on pain of death. Terror once more engulfed my heart and I realized I had to get out of the city the next day, a city where there were no longer any Jews. My hosts did everything they could to make my stay in their home as comfortable as possible, but I feared that if I were to stay I might bring tragedy upon the Hardaga family.'

So Kabilio turned to an acquaintance, who smuggled him out of Sarajevo to rejoin his family in the Italian zone. This time it was worth risking the journey. To stay would have been the greater danger. At the end of the war, the Kabilios returned to the city and were warmly welcomed by their Muslim protectors. 'The jewellery that we had left in their home', Yosef noted, 'was returned to us in the same box we had packed it in.' Of the 10,000 Jews in Sarajevo early in 1941, representing about ten per cent of the city's population, only 2,400 survived the war, fleeing like the Kabilios to the Italian zone. Most of the survivors emigrated to Israel after the establishment of the Jewish state in 1948.

Kabilio and his family settled in Jerusalem, where Yosef died in 1989 in his ninety-second year. On the strength of his testimony, Israel honoured the Hardaga family in June 1985. Zayneba, by then widowed, attended the Yad Vashem ceremony. The floor of the Ohel Yizkor, the Hall of Remembrance, is studded with the names of twenty-two Nazi concentration camps. Zayneba placed flowers on Jasenovac, where her father had met his death.

• • •

Selahattin Ulkumen, the thirty-year-old Turkish Consul in Rhodes, had reason to take German threats seriously even before he saved forty-two of the Greek island's Sephardi Jews from deportation to Auschwitz. By February 1944, Rhodes was the only Turkish mission still functioning in Axis-controlled territory. After Italy, which had ruled the Dodecanese chain since 1912, withdrew from the war in September 1943, the German army moved in. Turkey, which had remained neutral for the first four years of hostilities, started political and military talks with the British. The

Germans feared that a second front would be opened through the Aegean Sea with the help of the Turks. They played the bully.

'Our representation was closed in Bulgaria and Greece [Ulkumen explained in Tel Aviv forty-six years later]. All our missions were closed at the demand of the Germans. They also asked us to close the consulate in Rhodes. Turkey objected. We said if you insist that we close the consulate in Rhodes, we shall close your consulate in Smyrna. They didn't agree. Rhodes was the only consulate left to us in Axis-controlled territory. There was a very nervous atmosphere with the Germans in Rhodes. They wanted to intimidate Turkey. On 18 February 1944, two German 'planes bombed the consulate building. My wife was very seriously injured. She died six or seven months later after giving birth to our son.'

On 20 July 1944, the Gestapo ordered all of the island's 1,800 Jews to report to military headquarters for registration. They were descended from Jews expelled from Spain in 1492. Although they had lived under the Turkish and Italian Empires, they continued to speak Ladino, a Jewish dialect of medieval Spanish. The Jews of Rhodes were a tightly knit community, living in their own quarter of the old, Crusader town. Some had sought spouses among fellow Sephardim on the Turkish mainland. Ulkumen heard that all the Jews, regardless of nationality, were being herded together. A handful were Turkish citizens. He realized that they were to be sent to concentration camps:

'I went to the commander – General von Kleeman – and asked him to release forty-two Turkish citizens, who were Jewish by religion. Where a Turk was married, for example to an Italian, I said for humanitarian reasons that the whole family was Turkish. I succeeded in saving forty-two persons. Not all of them were Turkish. I don't know how many were not Turks. If I could, I would have saved more Jews, but it was beyond my competence. The forty-two were released, but the other Jews were conducted to Auschwitz.

'The German commander said that, according to Nazi laws, all Jews in their eyes were Jewish and had to go to concentration camps because Germany needed more manpower. I knew what their real purpose was – to kill them in the gas chambers. I objected. I said that, according to Turkish law, we didn't differentiate between whether a citizen was Jewish, Christian or Muslim. According to Turkish law, all citizens are equal. I convinced him. I said that I would advise my Government and that it would cause an international incident. Then he agreed.'

Asked how much he had to fear, from the Germans or his own Government, Ulkumen answered that he had acted out of conscience. That had been enough.

Of more than 1,700 Jews transported from Rhodes to Auschwitz, only 161 returned. Most of them subsequently settled in Israel. A square in the old Jewish quarter was renamed Platia Evreon Martyron (Square of the Hebrew Martyrs). The light, airy synagogue became a place of pilgrimage, but seldom of prayer. Matilda Turiel and her two sons were among the forty-two saved by the Consul. She had been born in Turkey, but had married a Jew from Rhodes who held Italian citizenship and had acquired his nationality. Having taken her husband, the Germans ordered her to come with her sons to Gestapo headquarters. If she refused, her husband would be killed. Ulkumen, whom she had never met before, intercepted them on the way and urged them not to enter the building. He took up their case. The family survived and settled in New York. Matilda Turiel flew to Jerusalem in June 1990, when the former Consul became the first Turk, and one of the rare Muslims, to be honoured by Yad Vashem.

At the beginning of August 1944, Turkey severed diplomatic and economic relations with Germany. Ulkumen and his wounded wife were interned. The Germans would not let them leave, but moved them to the Greek mainland. He returned to Turkey on VE day, 8 May 1945. 'Until then,' he said, 'I hadn't heard any news, but then I heard that all the Turkish Jews had escaped from Rhodes to the Turkish mainland. The forty-two had not been touched.'

After the war, Ulkumen continued his diplomatic career, serving in Europe, then as Consul-General in Beirut and Cairo. Afterwards, he was Deputy Secretary-General of CENTO, the now forgotten Central Treaty Organization. His son followed him into the foreign service and became a United Nations official in Geneva. Selahattin Ulkumen, who retired to Istanbul at the age of sixty-five, never remarried.

Asked whether anything in his personal history impelled him to risk life and liberty to save Jews, he told me, 'I didn't know the

Rhodes Jews. I had had no dealings with them. In Turkey I had Jewish friends, in the university. I didn't make any differentiation whether they were Jews or Muslims. I didn't ask what their religion was. I had no special ties with Jews. I only had humanitarian feelings to every human being. If they had been black people, I would have done the same thing.'

• ● •

Moshe Mandil was a photographer, the son-in-law of a photographer, the father of a photographer and the grandfather of a photographer. It was his trade that brought the Serbian Jew, his wife, son and daughter to share a room over an Albanian cowshed with another refugee family for ten precarious months in 1944. His Muslim host was the father of a photographer, and eventually the father-in-law and grandfather of photographers.

The story began in Mandil's Yugoslav home town, Novi Sad. After the German invasion in 1941, all the Jews were rounded up and transported to concentration camps. Moshe Mandil and his family went into hiding, then fled to the south of the country, which was under Italian occupation. The Italians put them in the Prishtina prison camp until March 1942, then exiled them to Albania. Along with about 150 other Yugoslav Jews, they were confined to the town of Kavaja. Every morning they had to report to the police.

When Mussolini capitulated in September 1943, and the Germans took over, it became very dangerous to stay in Kavaja. 'Everyone knew we were Jewish Yugoslav refugees,' Moshe's son, Gavra, told me in July 1990. 'There were five families of us living in the same house, each family to a single room. There were other Jewish families elsewhere in the town.' So the Mandils moved on. Disguised as Muslims, with Gavra's mother wearing a veil, they made their way to the capital, Tirana.

Moshe began to look for a studio, where he could earn enough money to feed his family. His eye fell on a sign reading 'Photo Neshad'. Moshe's father-in-law, Gavra Confino, had been photographer to the royal court of Serbia and had had an assistant called Neshad. It turned out to be the same man, an Albanian Muslim, a bachelor now in his thirties. Neshad offered Moshe space in his studio and packed the entire family into his home.

Moshe adopted Neshad's seventeen-year-old assistant, another Muslim called Refik Veseli, as his apprentice.

'They worked together [said Gavra Mandil]. My father took portraits of German officers while hiding under the black cloth. Refik moved the lights and generally helped. A great friendship developed. This lasted for five or six months in Tirana, from September 1943 to the beginning of 1944. Then the Germans were informed that there were Jewish refugees around. They started house-to-house searches. It became very, very dangerous to live there. Neshad was very scared. It was a great risk to keep us.'

Refik Veseli, who also lived in Neshad's house, took up the story. One day he answered a knock and found a German search party on the doorstep: 'I felt very shaky. The Jews not only looked different, they didn't speak our language. I said everyone here was Albanian. We could hear screams from the house opposite, where the Germans had seized a Jewish family.'

Refik got away with it that time, but it was the last straw. He and Neshad had already been debating what to do next. Now he knew that the Jews could not stay in Tirana. Refik's father, Vesel Veseli, a former teacher who had become an agent for a school stationery firm, happened to come into town on business from his home in the mountain village of Kruja. He stayed with Refik's older brother, Hamid. The photographer's apprentice consulted his father and brother:

'How could we save them? The question whether we should save them never arose. The only question was how to get them to the village. It was too dangerous by car, so we decided to go by donkey. Why did we take the risk? Our people had been underdogs for generations. All Albanians had been oppressed: by the Serbs, by the Austro-Hungarians, by the Turks, by the Italians, and now by the Germans. We were used to being under occupation. It was in our blood to help whoever suffered. Every child knew it was risky to help Jews, but help was a natural action. We saved only a few Jews. Others saved more.'

Vesel Veseli went back to the village, then returned with donkeys and pantaloons to disguise the Jews as Muslims. Moshe Mandil asked to bring another Jewish family, the Ben-Yosefs, with them. Vesel agreed. Gavra, then aged eight, remembered the trek:

'We travelled about three days and nights. During the day we hid in caves to avoid lorries and patrols. Kruja, where Refik's parents lived, was a small village, about ten to fifteen houses on very steep, rocky hills. Vesel owned a smallholding, a few olive trees and a couple of cows, but only for the family's own needs. There were four Mandils and three Ben-Yosefs. We mixed with Vesel's extended family. We shared a room over a cowshed. The adults had to stay in the room, but we kids mixed with the other children. Nobody noticed two more or less. The adults went out for fresh air only at night. Refik's father had never seen us before he took us to his place. As soon as Refik said we have to hide these people, he agreed. He knew the risk he was taking.'

During the ten months the Jews were there in 1944, Albanian partisans twice captured Kruja and twice lost it back to the Germans. It was a mixed blessing for the Mandils and the Ben-Yosefs. During the first two or three days of partisan control, the adults broke cover. They could walk and breathe by day as well as by night, but the neighbours started to ask questions. Vesel was indiscreet. Soon the whole village knew that he was hiding refugees. He assured his guests that they had nothing to worry about. 'They won't get to you before they get to me,' he told them. 'If they get to you, it will be over my dead body.' Forty-six years later, his son, Refik, told me, 'We are very proud that in Albania no Jews were betrayed by Albanians. After the partisans invaded, all of Kruja knew that we were hiding Jews. When the Germans came back, nobody betrayed us. Some even came to warn us when the Germans were coming.' But the second time the Germans took the village, Vesel decided he could not risk it again. So he rustled up the donkeys and took the two Jewish families back to the capital, where Refik had gone to join the resistance. They arrived, Gavra Mandil remembered, just in time for the battle of Tirana, seventeen days of house-to-house combat.

'We ran from house to house [he said], getting away from the Germans to the partisans. Refik fought in this battle. After seventeen days all was quiet. The streets were full of bodies and dead horses. Slowly, people came out of hiding.'

The Jews could stop running. At the beginning of 1945, Moshe Mandil took his wife, son and daughter back home to Yugoslavia. Before leaving he apologized to Refik for not having completed his apprenticeship. He invited him to join him in Novi Sad, where he reopened a studio. Borders were still open. In 1946, Refik took up his offer. He stayed with the Mandils in Novi Sad for eighteen months, returning to Albania in September 1947, after Moshe had taught him all he knew. He ran his own studio for nearly twenty years. When the Communists closed all private businesses, he became official photographer to the national museum. He married Drita, also a photographer, and their two sons followed them into the trade.

In December 1948, the Mandil family emigrated to Israel. Gavra, too, went into photography. Although Albania became the most repressive of Communist societies, closed not only to Israel but also to almost the entire world, the two families kept in touch and exchanged photographs. Refik called his first grandson Ron, the same name as Gavra's son, his old teacher's grandson. In July 1990, Refik and his wife came to Israel to be honoured at Yad Vashem – and to attend Ron Mandil's wedding.

6

An Act of Resistance

'If there are ten righteous Gentiles in the world,' wrote the fighting poet, Abba Kovner, 'Ona Simaite is one of them.' Ona Simaite, a Lithuanian librarian who was forty-two when the Germans took Vilna, was one of those for whom rescuing and succouring Jews was an act of resistance to the Nazi occupation. She and others like her – a tram driver, a barber, a housewife, a scout leader, a surgeon, a peasant, the head of a child welfare organization, a schoolmistress, the fathers of a future Foreign Minister of France and a future Prime Minister of Hungary, the grandfather of a film star – were fighting the Reich by frustrating the Final Solution. They were insisting on judging for themselves the humanity of the Jew, his place in Europe, his right to life. 'My father didn't save Jews,' the barber's son told me. 'He saved his friends.' They were repudiating a callous consensus decreed by the conqueror: good Aryans were not supposed to have Jewish friends. They were refusing to look the other way. In countries like Poland and Lithuania, with the largest Jewish communities in Europe and long indigenous traditions of anti-Semitism, they were risking the wrath not only of the Gestapo but also of their neighbours, some of whom joined in the slaughter while others were content with the pickings.

Ona Simaite had been taught by her working-class Lithuanian grandfather not to believe the slanders she heard about the Jews. He gave her books to read which showed them in a positive light. In October 1941, immediately after 80,000 Jews of Vilna were thrust into a ghetto, she and the director of the city library went to see what conditions were like and how they could help. A Jewish survivor, Tanya Sternthal, testified that she came back to the ghetto gates almost every day:

'She carried out life-sustaining errands and missions for hundreds of Jews who were strangers to her. She went to their Christian neighbours and asked them to hand over clothing and other valuables which the Jews had left behind – then returned them to their owners. More than once she was cursed by the "good Christians", who in their hearts waited for the destruction of the goods' owners. It was not an easy mission, and when she succeeded she was overjoyed. More than once the goods she restored saved their owners from dying of starvation.'

Ona Simaite lived on potatoes and cabbage. She used the rest of her rations to bring bread, grain, jam, scraps of cheese and margarine to the children in the ghetto orphanage. At the same time, she strove to salvage the Jewish heritage of Vilna, one of the great East European centres of Yiddish culture and learning. She collected books from Jewish libraries and hid them under the floor of her home. She preserved the books and manuscripts of the poet, Avraham Sutzkever. She brought whatever documents, genuine or forged, she could into the ghetto. Somehow, she managed to get identity papers and ration cards for a Jewish university lecturer who was hiding outside. She was a one-woman news service, keeping the Jews informed of what was happening in the world at large, and telling people outside what was going on in the ghetto. Another survivor, Sarah Nishmit, called her 'the life's breath of the ghetto'. With every visit, she put her life in danger.

When the ghetto was attacked, by gangs of Lithuanian and Latvian anti-Semites as well as by the Germans, she smuggled Jews to her home and hid them. Tanya Sternthal was one of them:

'She took me to her room and into her bed. I was a stranger to her, but she took care of me like a mother to a child in misery. Afterwards, when the Germans discovered the hiding-place and by some miracle did not take me away, Ona Simaite moved me to Keilis, where remnants of the Jews of Vilna were hiding, and continued to take care of me.'

A few days before the liquidation of the Vilna ghetto, Simaite brought out a ten-year-old girl and registered her as her niece. The false papers, which she had arranged through a lawyer, did not fool the Gestapo. Simaite was arrested and condemned to death, but her friends from the university, where she worked cataloguing books, bribed the Nazis to commute the sentence. She spent the rest of the war in a concentration camp in France, where she settled after the liberation into a life of solitary, impoverished exile. Jews she had helped during the war encouraged her to move to Israel in 1965, but it did not work out and she returned to Paris and went into an old-age home. According to a postcard received by Yad Vashem, which honoured her in 1967, she died peacefully in 1970, having willed her body to science.

• ● •

Like his father before him, Stanislaw Dutkievicz worked on the Warsaw tramways. They were a family of Catholic Socialists. His father sang in the church choir. Stanislaw grew up among Jews and Christians in the working-class district of Wola. Before the war, his parents used to visit Jewish friends and eat gefilte fish on Jewish feast days. When the Germans occupied the Polish capital in 1939 and ordered Jews into a ghetto, his friends turned to him for help. Two tram lines ran through the ghetto. Stanislaw, then aged twenty, had a pass to go in and out, driving or repairing trams. 'Unlike today, when you expect a reward,' he explained half a century later, 'you helped in those days because you grew up with these people. You went to school together, you played together and scrapped together when you were kids. The most tragic thing I saw in the war years was when the Germans caught Jewish kids with food. They hit them, banged them against the wall, killed them. After the war, I needed therapy to get over the shock of it all.'

At first, when some Jews were still living outside the ghetto, Dutkievicz maintained contact between members of divided families. He smuggled some of their possessions into the ghetto. 'When you had a pass, and you bribed the guards,' he told me, 'nobody asked questions.' As the situation deteriorated, with more and more Jews dying in the overcrowded ghetto, Dutkievicz was approached by two leaders of the Jewish underground, Tuvia Bozikovski and Stefan Grajek. Without hesitation, he agreed to help:

'There were hiding-places in the trams where we could put food supplies for the ghetto – potatoes, things like that. In the ghetto there were people who jumped on the tram and threw the supplies out. In the same way, we smuggled in guns, ammunition and grenades. Another resistance group was buying arms from German soldiers. I was in the group which distributed and smuggled them. They were also buying arms from Hungarian soldiers. They also stole guns from any soldier they spotted walking alone, or riding on a tram.'

On the return journey, he smuggled out Jews and found hiding-places for them with his mother and family friends. Some of those who came out of the ghetto could pass for Poles. The resistance issued them with forged papers and found them a place to stay. Dutkievicz smuggled the more Semitic-looking fugitives to the partisans. Bozikovski and Grajek constructed bunkers, concealed behind heating stoves, in two abandoned apartments which were in different streets. Up to twelve Jews could stay in each of the bunkers. Some stayed for two or three weeks, others longer. Another resistance group found them more permanent hiding-places. Dutkievicz's job was to bring in food to keep them alive, but he was soon playing a more active, and more perilous, role:

'Sometimes when the bunkers were full, more people came who needed shelter. I took them to the houses of my mother or my sister, where I hid them in the basement. My sister had a ground-floor flat. When the flow kept coming, Stefan Grajek helped us to buy a house. Through that we channelled Jews towards the partisans. Stefan also came to my wife and got her to help. We hid Jews in our house and had to feed them out of our own income.'

Grajek and Bozikovski themselves stayed with Dutkievicz and his wife, Czeslawa, for several months. 'They, of course, were endangering their lives,' Grajek wrote afterwards. 'There was no financial compensation for what they did. At certain periods representatives of the Jewish underground visited us there.'

Dutkievicz had no illusions about the danger they all faced. 'There were warning notices posted everywhere,' he said. 'The police made spot checks and searched houses. If I had been caught, I and my whole family would have been shot.' During the Warsaw ghetto uprising in the spring of 1943, he assisted Jews to escape through the sewers to the partisans. By his own estimate, he helped to save 200 Jews altogether. He continued working on the trams till 1943, when the Gestapo first came looking for him. His mother-in-law answered the door and told them that he was not at home. When they said that he was 'a bandit, a very dangerous man', she promised that, 'If ever he comes back, I'll let you know.' Dutkievicz went underground immediately and joined the resistance full-time. He did not go back. The Germans caught him four times all the same. He managed to escape three times while being transferred from one prison to another.

'The fourth time [he remembered], it was 1944. I was imprisoned in a transit camp, where they decided whether to send people to death, to a concentration camp, or to forced labour. I was sent to Germany. On the way I escaped when the train stopped at Lodz station. I told my guards I wanted to go to the lavatory. A German policeman went with me and stood outside. I noticed that the policeman was looking the other way. A passenger train was going past very slowly back towards Warsaw. I jumped on to this other train. I opened the door and climbed on to the roof. I lay down and waited until it reached the next stop at a small town thirty-five kilometres away. As it slowed down, I jumped on to the buffers and ran away.'

Later that year, he fought in the general Warsaw uprising. 'By then,' he said, 'it was too late to save any more Jews.'

· ● ·

Wladislawa Choms, the wife of a Polish army officer, started fighting for Jews before the Second World War. As an admirer of the Zionist idea, she had visited Palestine with her husband in 1934. When Polish university students launched a campaign of violence against Jews, Mrs Choms, a leading figure in the Democratic Party in Lvov, wrote critical articles for the local press and addressed meetings in support of the Jews. An Israeli survivor, Brunia Roth, heard her speak in 1937 at the grave of a Jewish student, who had been murdered by his anti-Semitic contemporaries:

'I remember Mrs Choms – dressed in black, a voice full of emotion – calling upon Polish mothers to make their sons cast the murderous knives from their hands and turn away from bloodshed. Polish university students nicknamed her the "Mother of the

Jews", and often warned her that she had enemies, but she paid no attention to the warnings and went on working for the welfare of the Jews.'

Lvov was invaded first by the Russians, then by the Germans. After the war, it became part of the Soviet Union. When the Russians entered the city, Mrs Choms organized Russian language classes for Jews so that they would be able to find jobs. She herself had to leave her apartment to evade the Soviet police, who were rounding up the wives of Polish officers and sending them to Siberia. When the Germans entered Lvov in June 1941, they arrested her husband. Her son escaped to England, where he joined the Royal Air Force. Wladislawa Choms organized a group of Poles to help the Jews. They found them hiding-places and provided them with forged papers. They collected gold and jewellery from the richer Jews and sold them to help their poorer brethren. When 70,000 Jews were confined in a ghetto, Mrs Choms and her friends smuggled in weapons and food and brought out Jewish children, who were placed in monasteries and orphanages. They also persuaded Polish families to foster sixty Jewish babies. In August 1942, Mrs Choms rescued two sisters after the rest of their family had been murdered. One of them, Ludmila Bogdanovich, who settled in Haifa after the liberation, recalled:

'She got us out of the ghetto, arranged papers for us and directed us to her friends in Zelinka, near Warsaw, who, thanks to Mrs Choms, assisted us throughout the war. When the time came that we had nothing to eat, since the Nazis had confiscated all our property, Mrs Choms arranged financial aid for us, enough for us to live modestly. When I fell ill with typhus, she brought a doctor to me, for no money, and he saved me from death's door.'

The Jews called her the 'Angel of Lvov'. Although no one can know how many she saved, Brunia Roth testified that many people all over the world owed their lives to her:

'Some didn't even know who the angel guarding over them was, because she acted in silence, through the underground, to prevent the Germans from finding out about her activities. When someone fell ill, she tried to get medicine and money for them. She asked everyone to let her know about any unprotected Jewish soul. She would listen to Allied broadcasts, translate the news into Polish, then type bulletins. I would distribute them among those who were aware of the political situation and who would be happy to get a hint of hope for a better future. She herself had to go into hiding, to endure hunger and cold, in order to go on helping others.'

By 1943, Lvov had become too hot for Mrs Choms because the Germans were on her trail. She fled to Warsaw. At the end of the war, she left Poland to look for her husband, who had been imprisoned in France, and her son. She learned for the first time that her son had died on active service. Her husband survived, only to die after a long and painful struggle against cancer. When she came to Jerusalem in March 1963, she was living in an old-age home in London. Ludmila Bogdanovich, who had traced her there, discovered that 'she had been living in harsh conditions for a long while and had worked twenty hours a day to sustain her husband and herself during the period he was mortally ill'. She was too proud to accept financial help from those she had saved. After planting a tree at Yad Vashem, Wladislawa Choms, the 'Mother of the Jews', the 'Angel of Lvov', said, 'This is the first ray of light in my life since the end of the war, and I stand here on the Mount of Remembrance with feelings of happiness and shame.' Happiness at what she had achieved, shame that it had ever been necessary.

• • •

For Henryk Grabowski, a Polish scout leader in his early twenties, the Jews were not helpless victims, but comrades-in-arms. He was the contact man between the militant young Zionists of the Jewish Fighting Organization and the Polish underground. He was the first to bring the news of mass executions from Vilna to Warsaw, and of armed resistance from Warsaw to Vilna. He procured, concealed and smuggled guns, knives and explosives into the Warsaw ghetto. He guided Jews out. His home on the Aryan side served as a safe-house for Jewish fighters. He plucked a Jewish prisoner from under the noses of the Gestapo. 'Co-operation in struggle brought people closer,' he reflected. 'Young Poles and young Jews found friendship. Each was ready to give his life for the other.'

Rumours filtered through to Warsaw in the summer of 1941 that the Germans were slaughtering Jews wholesale in the major eastern centres of Vilna, Bialystok and Lvov and confiscating their property. The 400,000 Jews crammed into the Warsaw ghetto were reluctant to believe them. They were demoralized and disorientated. Against all the current evidence, they still pinned hopes of survival on a Nazi defeat on the battlefield. The young fighters were among the few who took the stories seriously. So were Polish patriots like Grabowski, who argued that the Nazis would exterminate the Jews first, then the Poles. Grabowski attended a first meeting of Jewish and Polish fighters in the ghetto. They resolved to take up arms against the occupying power.

That autumn, Yosef Kaplan of the Socialist Zionist Hashomer Hatzair youth movement and Irena Adamowicz of the Polish scouts dispatched Grabowski to Vilna to rally support for organized resistance, to order existing groups to gather intelligence on troop and civilian movements, and to cultivate sources in the local and railway police forces. To reach Vilna he had to cross two de facto borders. The 230-mile journey took him two weeks, and he rode the last lap on a freight train with the connivance of Polish workers. He had to evade frequent checkpoints, manned by vicious Lithuanian and Latvian police auxiliaries who thought nothing of shooting anyone who aroused the slightest suspicion.

In Vilna the 'actions', which disposed of 60,000 Jews out of a total of 80,000 in three or four months, were under way. As the gas chambers were not yet in operation, the Jews were taken out and shot. Grabowski was received on the Aryan side by Chaika Grossman, who slipped him into the ghetto. 'His arrival', she said, 'symbolized the first break through the ring of isolation and total absence of communication surrounding the Vilna ghetto.' He found the Jewish youth movements already organizing for resistance. He urged them to work in harness with the Lithuanian underground, in which the scout movement again was prominent, and to co-ordinate as best they could with Warsaw.

Before trekking back to the Polish capital, Grabowski went to see for himself whether the stories of mass executions were true. Accompanied by Jadwiga Dudziec, a Lithuanian scout and resistance heroine, he cycled into the countryside. Between Vilna and Trok they came upon a party of 300–400 Jews toting bundles and dragging small children behind them. They were led in batches into the forest, where Grabowski saw ten of the hated auxiliaries digging trenches. He managed to exchange a few words with one of the groups, urging them to flee rather than to face execution. The Jews told him that they were being sent to dig potatoes. They did not want to believe him. Soon two or three trucks arrived with about twenty soldiers under the command of an SS officer. 'The victims put their belongings on one side,' he reported, 'stripped to their underwear, then were body-searched and shot beside the newly dug pits.'

The next morning, Grabowski and Jadwiga hired a kayak for a 'fishing trip' and paddled across a lake towards Tyszkiewicz castle, which was under German military occupation. Their intention was to gather information on who was using it and for what purpose. They could not get very close, but they could see troops milling around and about 500 civilians with bundles of clothes. They concluded, Grabowski wrote later, that this was another group of Jews being led to the slaughter:

'We hid in the rushes. We could hear the auxiliaries and the Germans shouting orders and the cries of the civilians getting ready for execution. They were shot with semi-automatic weapons. We also heard single shots. That was to finish off any who were still alive. The executions took about three hours. When the guns fell silent, we waited to see what would happen next. Soon we saw drunken auxiliaries leading out three horse-drawn carts filled with clothes, bedding and other small items. These were the same men who had taken part in the executions. Now their aim was to sell the booty in Trok. But nobody among the townspeople came out to buy. The drunken auxiliaries were so incensed by this that they set the wooden houses on fire, then flung the clothes off the carts. Two SS officers arrived by motorcycle and ordered the auxiliaries back to the castle. By the next day, the fires had burned down. Everything fell quiet. The SS and the auxiliaries left the castle. Gradually, people came back to their homes. Life returned, but it was life without joy.'

It was in Vilna that Grabowski first met Arieh ('Jurek') Wilner, who was to become his Jewish brother-in-arms, the Warsaw ghetto's man on the outside. The fair-haired Wilner looked like a true Aryan, Grabowski noted, though he was still not at ease in the part. They attended mass together in a Catholic church, but Wilner genuflected at the wrong times and mixed up the prayers. A Polish contemporary described him as 'quiet, self-controlled, clever, ready for anything, a cheerful smile always on his lips, a man who aroused confidence in all with whom he came in touch'. Back in Warsaw, Wilner moved into Grabowski's home. Grabowski supplied him with explosive materials, grenades, knives and brass knuckles for the ghetto fighters. His house became a postbox for packages and money arriving from the ghetto.

When the traffic began to arouse suspicion, Wilner moved into an empty apartment. Unknown to him, it was under surveillance because a member of the Polish resistance had lived there before him. He came home one day and was jumped by six Gestapo men, who thought that they had captured a Polish fighter. He was interrogated and tortured on that assumption. The Gestapo demanded names and other details about the structure and arms of the Polish underground. When he could no longer stand the pain, Wilner 'confessed' that he was a Jew. They beat him again, demanding to know how he had escaped from the ghetto and where he had acquired the arms found in his apartment. Wilner insisted that he was operating alone, seeking to avenge his murdered parents. The interrogators soon lost interest, transferring him first to the Pawiak prison, then to the Rembertow forced labour camp on the outskirts of Warsaw.

With the help of a sympathetic guard, Wilner smuggled a note to Grabowski, urging his Polish friends to get him out. 'Despite everything,' Wilner wrote, 'I did not lose my life.' The Poles suspected a Gestapo trap, but Grabowski went to check on the spot. The camp, he found, was an old brickworks housing about 500 Jews. He tried, unsuccessfully, to catch a glimpse of Wilner on his way to work. The next day, he came back and went straight to the guardhouse, where he complained that Wilner had been a tenant of his and had left without paying the rent. Times were hard, he explained, and he needed the money.

'After a while [he wrote three years after the war] they brought Jurek. He was emaciated, wounded and beaten, but his face already had a normal look. He recognized me from afar and threw his arms around me. I wasn't too pleased with that. I embraced him, but at the same time winked at him and scolded him, "Why did you live with me, then leave without paying the money for the room?" But Jurek didn't understand a thing. "What money?" he asked. So I repeated, "Don't play the fool, let me have the money you owe me, otherwise I'll have to notify the Gestapo." Jurek didn't understand the situation at all. He thought I had been arrested. To try to make him understand, I said, "I came here today especially to get the money, I must get it." Finally he understood. I left, threatening that in the evening I'd come back for the money.'

Grabowski returned that evening, hoping to catch the prisoners on their way back from work and somehow to distract the guards so that Wilner could get away, but he had missed them. The camp was on the edge of a swamp. At 8 p.m., with only one hour left before the night curfew came into force, he picked his way through the marshland.

'With difficulty,' he wrote, 'I managed to reach the barracks. I dragged out Jurek, who was very weak and could barely move. But we got beyond the perimeter of the camp.' It was a quarter to nine, too late to make it back to Grabowski's home, so he took Wilner to a friend, who, 'not very willingly', let him stay till morning. They reached Grabowski's home at 5 a.m. Grabowski kept Wilner there for ten days, feeding him and treating him with home-made medicine. Then Wilner insisted on returning to the ghetto, where, despite the effects of the Gestapo torture, he fought, and died, in the uprising of April 1943.

· ● ·

Leonard Glinski is the man, quoted in the prologue, who 'saved one life'. He was born at Kartuzy, near Gdansk, in 1917 and studied law at Warsaw University. He was in the capital under the German occupation from 1939 to 1944. His singular act of compassion was a by-product of his work in an underground resistance group affiliated to the Polish Home Army. Unlike most of the other rescuers in this chapter, he had no particular link with the Jews. He saw an individual in distress, and he had to do something about it. When we met in 1989, he was a spry seventy-two year old, recently retired from a post-war career as a foreign trade economist and translator (he spoke English, German and Spanish and had spent much of his business life in Arab states).

In 1943, the time of the mass deportation of Jews from Polish ghettos to extermination camps, Glinski worked in the office of a road building and repairing firm, which was also a cover for the resistance. He used to go home with his boss every evening for dinner. One night he noticed a new face there, a fourteen-year-old girl:

'My chief had a big flat. The girl was sitting in a very small room with a small window. Nobody could look in. It was very dangerous to keep Jews in private flats. I saw the girl, whose name was Alina Pottock, for one or two weeks, always in this room. She was a girl without papers, without money. After a couple of weeks, my chief told me it was becoming dangerous to keep her. Some neighbours had heard there was a Jewish girl in his flat. He was afraid for his family.'

Alina had escaped to Warsaw from the ghetto in Bedzin, her home town in Silesia. Her father was in Russia with the Polish army and had lost contact with his wife and daughter. The Nazis gave Alina a permit to accompany supply trucks out of the ghetto because she spoke German and Polish. One day she heard from the Germans that the ghetto was to be liquidated. She urged her mother to go with her on a truck and escape under the tarpaulin, but her mother refused to leave. Alina fled on her own, taking a train to Warsaw. She remembered the name and address of Glinski's boss, who was also from Silesia and knew her parents. She knocked at his door and asked for help. He took her in, but after two weeks was close to panic. He asked Glinski and other resistance men what they could do.

'I saw the girl was in great danger. I said, "Give me two weeks, and I will find papers for her, a new name, a new age and so on." The Home Army had men in various offices. One of them could buy a blank identity card, signed and stamped by a German officer. All you had to do was fill it in by typewriter. I made her a photograph and bought special ink. She wrote her signature. We decided she should keep her name, but that she would be sixteen instead of fourteen (children couldn't have an identity card). At sixteen she could work. Through other sources, I arranged for her to be made a Catholic. I got a baptismal certificate from St Casimir's church in Lvov, which was then under Russian occupation. It was signed and stamped by a priest. I managed through the Home Army to arrange that she had studied at a secondary school in Warsaw.'

After consulting other underground people, Glinski arranged

for Alina to be sent to Vienna to work as a maid in a doctor's family. For the rest of the war, he kept in touch with her by post. 'Her letters were full of feeling,' he told me. 'She said she didn't know where her mother and father were, whether they were alive or dead.'

Glinski was arrested in his boss's apartment during the 1944 Warsaw uprising, but escaped from a transit camp where he had been sent for 'selection'. Alina's father came back with the conquering Red Army and advertised in the press asking anyone who knew of her fate to get in touch with Alina's uncle in Katowitz. Glinski took a 220-mile train ride to Silesia, found the uncle and gave him the Vienna address. The father went to Austria and brought Alina home.

'The uncle invited me to stay with him. After three or four days, her father arrived with Alina. She came into my room. She hugged me so hard I almost couldn't breathe. Her father offered me money, but I refused.'

Alina settled later in Sydney, Australia, where she married, had two sons and owned a travel agency. She kept in touch with Leonard Glinski, and in 1985 petitioned Yad Vashem to give him the medal that said if you saved one life, it was as if you had saved the whole world.

• • •

Witold Fomienko was a rare Polish Christian who spoke Yiddish. He was born in Warsaw in 1905, the son of a musician. He arrived in Lutsk, then eastern Poland, now part of the Ukraine, in 1924 with his father, an army bandsman. He made friends among the town's 18,000 Jews, learning to read and write their language. Young Witold followed his father into music, playing the clarinet and saxophone. Shortly before the war broke out in 1939, he began to suffer from heart trouble and his doctors advised him to stop playing. Nahum Sofer, a Jewish musician who also owned a barber shop, gave him a job and taught him the trade. Fomienko mixed even more with Jews. Some of his closest friends were members of the militant Betar Zionist youth movement, whose Polish leader at that time was Menachem Begin, a future Prime Minister of Israel. When the Germans invaded in 1941, Fomienko repaid his debt by opening his own barber shop and employing

Jewish staff. He also found work for other Jews with Polish barbers he knew.

Before long, however, the Jews were driven into a ghetto. Once again, he resolved to help his friends. He devised routes in and out of the ghetto, which, according to survivors, became his second home. Out of his own pocket he bought the Jews bread and other foodstuffs, medicines and firewood. He brought news of the outside world. Whatever they asked for, he tried to deliver. As the killings increased, Fomienko began to smuggle Jews out of the ghetto in a wagon and hid them in an apartment he had rented from a Polish Christian. He moved his parents into the apartment to provide cover for the fugitives. Fomienko's father would bring them food. One Christmas Eve, Witold brought all the hidden Jews to a party in his own apartment. He also collected and catalogued photographs left behind in the ghetto by murdered families.

Shoshana Jacobovitz was an eleven-year-old orphan when she first met him. Her parents and the rest of her family had been killed in the Lutsk ghetto. She had escaped to the nearby village of Podhajce, where young Jews were working as forced labourers on local farms. She was blonde and blue-eyed, looking, as she wrote later, 'like a typical Gentile'. Fomienko thought that she would be safer in town and hid her in his parents' home.

'Jews of all ages used to come there and ask for a place to sleep. It was almost a hotel, except that in a hotel they would have had to pay, and Witold's family asked for nothing. Instead of being concerned that by giving food and shelter to us he was endangering his own life and the lives of his family, he worried about the refugees who came to him, encouraged them, tried to raise their spirits, calmed them down and found them safe-houses among his Christian acquaintances. Sometimes Fomienko paid for lodgings with his own money. He promised the Christians anything if they would agree to hide the runaways.'

When Polish neighbours started informing on his Christian helpers, he roamed the streets of Lutsk day and night to warn the hidden Jews of the danger they were facing. Other Poles who had sheltered Jews and managed to elude the Gestapo came to him for advice. Once again he calmly found them temporary hideouts. In her contribution to a book compiled after the war by Lutsk survivors, Shoshana Jacobovitz concluded: 'I loved that family very much. They treated me very well and worried about me. If I managed to stay alive, it was thanks first and foremost to that family.'

Witold Fomienko and his parents saved about thirty-six Jews in their own apartments and helped hundreds more. They were assisted from the start by Ogenya Friedbaum, a Jewish girl whose brother had played with Witold in a band. After the liberation, Witold and Ogenya were married. They moved to Israel with their twelve-year-old son, Mark, in 1957. 'My mother and I didn't want to come to Israel,' Mark, by then the deputy manager of a bank in Ashkelon, confessed thirty-four years later. 'He did. He had friends here. He wanted to leave Poland.' Witold, who had already suffered a stroke, never worked in Israel. He died in 1961 and was buried in the Catholic cemetery in Ramle. 'Hundreds of weeping, mourning Jews', the Hebrew daily paper *Davar* recorded, 'walked behind the large cross which was borne after his coffin.'

• • •

Hospitals, like convents, offered infinite possibilities for concealment. They had their own mystique, their own hierarchies, their own vestments. They demanded a measure of respect, even of awe, from jackbooted intruders. The Gestapo could not simply stride in and wreak havoc. In Bratislava, a loose network of Slovakian doctors conspired with the resistance to rescue Jews and other fugitives. One of the most ingenious was a professor of urology, Dr Joseph Jaksy, who treated dozens of patients whose only 'sickness' was their presence on the Nazi hit list. As many as sixteen at a time slept in the wards and were given daily, but harmless, injections. Dr Jaksy sheltered a sixty-year-old Jewish woman for three years. She locked herself in a bathroom all day, coming out only at night. When shot-down Allied pilots were brought to him, the doctor put their jaws in casts so that they would not be able to speak if they were intercepted while being smuggled out of the country.

His most audacious coup was to whisk a Jew into the operating theatre when the Gestapo came looking for him. The man was hiding in the urology clinic until a more permanent refuge could be found. Dr Jaksy administered an anaesthetic and opened up the man's stomach, then told the Germans that it was impossible to take a patient off the table in the middle of an operation. By the time they came back for him, the man had gone. All Jewish males were vulnerable to 'trouser checks'. The doctor performed new operations to make it look as if they had only just been circumcized, then furnished papers testifying that the surgery had been necessary for medical reasons.

Alexander Eckstein, a Jew who was active in the underground, was rounded up for transportation to Auschwitz. While he was waiting at the assembly point, his wife, a doctor, arranged for Eckstein and two others to receive urgent medical examinations by Dr Jaksy. A German soldier escorted them to the hospital and left them there.

'Jaksy announced that he would be able to see me in about two hours [Eckstein wrote]. During that short period of time he managed to find me a hiding-place. My wife hid with the nurses. The other two Jews were also hidden. When the German soldier returned and did not find us, he started to run wild and Dr Jaksy replied coolly it seemed that the patients had escaped while the doctors were out and that they were not responsible for guarding the prisoner-patients. The soldier was no doubt afraid of being punished, so he kept quiet.'

Another time, Mrs Gizi Fleishman, who represented the American Jewish Joint Distribution Committee in Slovakia, was arrested. Before the Gestapo took her away, she passed about $20,000 and two million Czech crowns, destined for the Jewish underground, to Dr Jaksy. He handed every cent to Eckstein. The doctor also exploited his position as the personal physician of the mayor of Bratislava to smuggle food in the mayor's official car to a Jewish friend in hiding in Vienna. Early in the war, Dr Jaksy helped his first wife, a Jewess, to flee via Budapest to neutral Switzerland.

The professor's chief assistant and fellow conspirator was Dr Juraj Csiky, then in his early thirties. During the mass round-ups in 1942, he was on duty in the urology department when the Gestapo came calling:

'Two men in uniform and two in civilian dress ordered me to let them have all the Jewish patients. Since I guessed what would become of them, I tried with all my powers to save them. I did not hand over the patients – there were then sixteen of them – and I told the delegation that I had no authority to release the patients.

They would have to come back tomorrow, when the professor would be present. When the four men had left, I immediately told the patients what was going on and that they must leave the clinic that evening after six. In the morning, when the Germans returned, the patients were no longer in the hospital.'

For almost half a century, neither the professor nor his assistant talked about their rescue mission. Dr Jaksy rebuilt his practice in New York, where an Israeli-born psychotherapist, Amira Trattner, heard his story while treating him for Parkinson's disease in his old age. When she urged him to put his experiences on record, he replied, 'Wouldn't you do this for your neighbour?' He felt, she sensed, that it was almost shameful to talk about it. Dr Jaksy died aged ninety-one in the summer of 1991, three months after being honoured by both Israel and the state of New York. Another Israeli, Eliyahu Arbel, came across Dr Csiky in 1988 while on a return visit to his native Bratislava. The doctor had married the sister of Arbel's childhood friend and host. It turned out that he had treated Arbel's mother, who spent ten months in the urology clinic. 'What I did', he wrote to Yad Vashem, 'I did in my role as a doctor and out of my feelings as a human being.'

• • •

Alexa Puti would have taken the young Jew into his cottage, but he was worried that his daughter's hard-drinking boyfriend might give him away in one of his less discreet moments. Puti, an illiterate Romanian peasant, had befriended the Solomon family when he came to buy clothes from their factory in Somcuta Mare on market days. After the German invasion in 1939, the region was ceded to Hitler's Hungarian ally. The Jews were relatively safe until March 1944, when the Germans entered the town and began to register them as a preliminary to deportation. The Solomons and their friends the Barachs fled into the countryside, but then thought better of it and returned to the Somcuta Mare ghetto. Their twenty-two-year-old son, Jacob Solomon, alone chose to stay in the forest. It was then that he knocked on Alexa Puti's door in the village of Buteasa and asked him to help him hide because his life was in danger.

The peasant led Jacob to a tiny cave on the mountain near his home. Aided by his son, Todor, and daughter, Maria, he dug out the cave to a depth of about five feet and installed Jacob inside. To reach it up the rock face they had to climb a ladder, which the young Jew kept in the cave. The Putis brought him food three times a week. Knowing that he ate only kosher food, they made a point of fetching only vegetables and dairy produce.

'My existence and my hiding-place were kept a secret by them [Jacob wrote], even from their daughter's fiancé, since it was well known that he was a big drinker, and they feared that he might reveal the secret while drunk. They even took pains to buy me a newspaper every week. They didn't know how to read and write and every time they were asked why, they would say it was for the teacher in their village or for their priest.'

When the Gestapo realized that Jacob had not returned to the ghetto with his parents, they came looking for him with a posse of twenty-five Hungarian policemen. Luckily for him, they assumed that he would be deep in the forest and neglected to search so close to the village. Despite a decree that anyone caught hiding Jews would be deported, Alexa Puti and his family kept Jacob in a cave for five months. 'They made these efforts', he insisted, 'out of friendship and a desire to help me. Even if I gave them a small amount of money, it went for the food and clothing that were provided for me.'

Jacob Solomon settled in Israel in 1950 and lost touch with his saviours for almost thirty years. He revisited Romania in 1979 and 1983 and went back to the village. Alexa and Todor had died, but he re-established contact with Maria and Todor's children. Asked by Yad Vashem whether Maria was in financial need, Jacob replied, 'Her condition is just as it was in 1944. They eat potatoes, black bread and they have a goat.'

• • •

Soon after the mass deportation of Belgian Jews began in 1942, Yvonne Nevejean, director of l'Oeuvre National de l'Enfance, the national child welfare organization, was asked by the Belgian Jewish Defence Committee if she could find shelter for children whose parents feared that they would be sent east to the death camps. She accepted without hesitation. She did not consult her committee, sought no authorization and told no one what she was going to do. What she did, in an elaborate clandestine operation, was to place at least 3,000 of what became known as 'Yvonne's children' in the safety of foster homes, ONE orphanages or convent boarding-schools. When she was honoured by Israel in 1965, she responded that she had acted 'simply out of love for those who were suffering the most horribly during the German occupation'. She, in turn, praised the Jews of Belgium for their 'dignity and courage in those dark and depressing times', which she said 'made me never despair of human nature'. Before the war, Belgium had a Jewish population of about 66,000. The Nazis killed 26,000 of them.

Mme Nevejean's secretary was the only one who shared her secret in full. She kept separate files of the Jewish children, listing their new and old identities. Mme Nevejean sent out trusted associates to locate the children and bring them either to ONE transit camps or directly to safe-houses. The heads of convents or boarding-schools were told as much, or as little, as they needed to know. The Jewish parents were kept in ignorance of where their children had found refuge, though ONE couriers passed messages between them. Mme Nevejean obtained false identity cards for her charges. She supplied food ration coupons. Where people asked for money to cover board and lodging, she paid them with funds parachuted or smuggled in from London by agents of the Belgian government-in-exile. On the night of 30 October 1942, the Gestapo transferred fifty-eight Jewish children from a German-controlled orphanage to the Malines transit camp en route for Auschwitz. Mme Nevejean interceded with Queen Elisabeth, the mother of King Leopold and honorary president of ONE, who persuaded a German general to spare them.

It was claimed after the liberation that not one of 'Yvonne's children' was discovered by the Germans. The Gestapo suspected her of saving Jews and frequently raided her office and interrogated her. On one occasion, a senior Gestapo officer forced her to accompany him in a search of a children's home at Crainhem. He came away empty-handed, although more than a third of the children living there were Jewish. The proportions were often very high. At one of the homes, l'Institut d'Heverlee, there were 175 Jews out of a total of 600 children. Another, the Sacred Heart convent at Auderghem, hid sixty young Jews who had been rescued by a Jewish resistance squad from a showpiece government colony at Wezembeek. It was 1944, the eve of the Allies' Normandy invasion, and the resistance feared that the children would be deported. The convent turned one of its cellars into a dormitory. Mme Nevejean and ONE made sure that the children did not go hungry.

In August 1944, when Jewish defence groups learned that a senior Gestapo officer was coming to Brussels to finish off the last Jews left in the capital, they appealed to Mme Nevejean to save still more children. 'I can never forget the determination, the diligence, the heart with which Mme Nevejean applied herself to this task,' Marie Blum-Albert, one of the Jewish activists, testified. 'She was telephoning everywhere, to convents, to all kinds of hostels, to homes for war orphans and prisoners' children, doggedly pleading our cause before influential people and finally obtaining shelter for the children in homes that were already overcrowded.'

At Yvonne Nevejean's funeral in August 1987, a former member of the Jewish Defence Committee, Yvonne Jospa, said, 'She was committed, without reservation and despite all the dangers, to the rescue of Jewish children, motivated by her love of children, her ideological rejection of all forms of racism, her struggle against the Nazi occupation. Her principal hope was to give the Jewish children the same chance of survival and development as the non-Jewish children.'

On a smaller scale, but with no less commitment and courage, Alice Ferrières, a mathematics teacher in Murat, a small town in the south of France, was mothering fifteen Jewish teenage fugitives in a girls' boarding-school. With her comrades in the resistance, she also found staging-posts for hundreds more Jews fleeing the Germans. Most of the children had been sent south from Paris into the 'free zone' controlled by the Vichy French Government at the outbreak of war in September 1939. They were relatively safe so long as the Germans kept their distance, but in 1943 the Reich extended its control and the Jews had to go underground. Mlle Ferrières, a single woman aged about forty, was waiting for them.

Erna Stern, a seventeen-year-old German girl whose family moved to France when Hitler came to power in 1933, was one of her first protégées. She and two friends were sent to Murat with false names and papers identifying them as Protestants:

'Alice Ferrières reached out a hand to all who were fleeing the

Germans. Thanks to her enormous courage and her devotion, we were able to stay in the boarding-school, each placed in the class appropriate to his or her age, along with the non-Jewish pupils. In Mlle Ferrières's small apartment we were given not only extra food to supplement the meagre fare we received at the school, but more important a warm home, a veritable refuge.'

Another of her girls, Solange Factor, added that Mlle Ferrières made sure that each of them lit candles on Friday night, the sabbath eve, celebrated Jewish festivals and honoured their religious traditions. 'She endangered her very soul by taking care of us until the liberation and dedicated all of her free time to us.'

In the summer of 1944, fierce fighting broke out in the vicinity between the German army and the French resistance. At great personal risk, Alice Ferrières kept herself informed on Wehrmacht troop movements. As the occupying forces came closer and closer, she managed to smuggle the children to new havens in the countryside, without revealing their Jewish identity to the farming families who gave them shelter. The children returned to Murat when it was liberated by the resistance and stayed at the boarding-school until the end of the war. Mlle Ferrières adopted two Jewish orphans and brought them up until they were old enough to support themselves.

'I know that without her help during the war years I would probably not be here,' Solange Factor wrote twenty years later, when Alice Ferrières was honoured by Israel. 'My mother was deported in the summer of 1943, and that terrible period would have been much more difficult to bear. The prime quality in that woman's heart was unfettered love, and she dedicated her whole being to rescuing people.'

• • •

Simone Nathan, a Jewish schoolgirl, was in her last year of lycée when she was set an essay on loyalty. It was to be written in the form of a letter to Marshal Pétain, whose Vichy regime still ruled central France in early 1943 as a puppet of the Germans. Since Pétain's Government had confiscated all her father's property because he was a Jew, she wrote what she described later as an 'explosive' letter. The headmistress was scandalized and warned Simone that the school would do nothing to help if she was called to account. She had no choice but to leave. It was then that her parents turned to Georges Dumas, a leader of the resistance in their home town of Limoges and father of the future Socialist Foreign Minister, Roland Dumas. Within two or three days, Georges Dumas placed the dissident schoolgirl as a boarder in a convent attached to a local hospital. Although he persuaded the hospital director to give her a *laissez-passer*, he advised her to go out as little as possible. On at least one occasion, Georges Dumas and his son visited the convent to make sure that she was not having too hard a time. In fact, the mother superior, Mother Sylvie, treated her with great affection.

Despite all the precautions, however, another boarder, a member of the Vichy militia, denounced her. Simone's parents turned again to Georges Dumas. By then the general situation in Limoges had deteriorated. Any Jew was liable to be arrested merely for being a Jew. Dumas obtained false identity papers for Simone, her father, mother and brother and found them a hiding-place in the country. He also saved other Jews, including Henri Sandler, a future president of the local Jewish community. He persuaded the Vichy authorities to release Sandler after he had been detained and threatened with death. In March 1944, Georges Dumas's luck ran out. He was arrested and executed by firing squad for his resistance activities.

Roland Dumas planted a tree at Yad Vashem in his father's memory during an official visit to Jerusalem in January 1989. Simone, now Mme Ascher, director of a Limoges art gallery, paid a personal tribute. In a twist of history, the tree was uprooted by a Jewish nationalist who objected to the Foreign Minister's dialogue with the Palestine Liberation Organization.

Joszef Antall was a less likely saviour of Jews. He was a head of department in the Hungarian Interior Ministry under the pro-Nazi regime of Admiral Horthy. While Georges Dumas's son became a Socialist Foreign Minister, Antall's (also Joszef) was elected a right-wing Prime Minister in Hungary's first post-Communist Government. Antall senior was responsible for Polish soldiers who fled to Hungary after the German invasion of September 1939. Before the Nazis seized control of Hungary in 1944, the Hungarians, for reasons of their own, helped many of the Poles to escape to Britain and to return to the ranks of the army in exile.

Hundreds of Polish Jewish fugitives grabbed the chance to evade the Gestapo by donning uniform and joining the refugees in Hungary with forged military papers. The Hungarian police knew who the Jews were, but on Interior Ministry orders did not challenge them. The Horthy administration, which collaborated with Hitler against its own Jewish citizens, angered the Germans by treating their Polish brethren differently. A second wave of Polish Jews escaped to Hungary during the deportation years of 1943–4. Again, Antall concealed their identities. His job was to sift all foreigners and send the Jews to forced labour in the Ukraine. Survivors affirmed that, even when he visited refugee camps and recognized Jews, he either did not check them, or he supplied them with Aryan papers.

He persisted with what had become a highly dangerous policy after the German occupation. He was arrested by the Gestapo and narrowly escaped execution. 'Hundreds, perhaps thousands, of Jews owed their life to him,' said Dr Gabriel Bar-Shaked, a Yad Vashem researcher into the fate of Hungarian Jewry. 'If he had wanted to do something against the Jews, he had the policy and the means. A lot of Hungarians did the opposite of what he did.'

• • •

Tantalizingly little is known about Halfdan Ullman's role in speeding Jews on their escape through the fjords of occupied Trondheim, but it cost the Norwegian professor his life. What follows, as a postscript to this chapter of rescue and resistance, is as much his granddaughter's story as his. Liv Ullman, the star of some of Ingmar Bergman's most celebrated films, never knew her grandfather. She was born in Japan. At the beginning of the war she was taken to Canada, where the air force trained her father along with other Norwegian émigré pilots. In the last weeks of the war, her father was killed in action. The telegram informing the family in Norway crossed with one recording the death of Halfdan in German captivity.

'For many years all we knew of my grandfather's last months on earth [Liv Ullman told me] was that he had been very active in the underground in occupied Norway, and when he had housed and helped Jews to flee Trondheim, he was taken as a hostage by the Germans. They first sent him to prison in Oslo, and later he was transported out of the country and rumoured to have been sent to Dachau. Through my childhood, many stories circulated how he was shot in Dachau, or how he had been made to carry heavy stones to exhaust him since he was an elderly man not in the best of health. Much effort was made to find out what his last days had been like, but to no avail.'

Years later, when Liv Ullman was twenty-five, she went to Poland on a cultural exchange. She was sitting in a café with some artists when a man came up to her and said, 'I hear your name is Ullman.' He paused a moment, then asked, 'Would you know of the family of Halfdan Ullman?' The actress replied that he was her grandfather.

'The Polish man had tears in his eyes and said, "This is very strange for me. I shared a bed with your grandfather in Dachau." Thus I learned about the life and death of this man I had never met but had heard so much about. He had been a comfort to everyone in his barracks because spiritually he was a very strong man, although his body was that of a wraith. He finally gave in to pneumonia which, of course, was untreated, and was not helped by his having to work carrying stones in the cutting fields. My grandfather's family will remember him for his life before this ending, as well as his honourable death, although I believe no deaths are honourable, only actions are.'

7

The Few Who Disobeyed

'I did little,' Hugo Armann, a sergeant-major in Hitler's army, said after planting a tree in the Avenue of the Righteous at Yad Vashem in September 1986, 'but if many had done their little, it would have added up to much.' Armann, a sixty-nine-year-old retired school principal when he came to Jerusalem, saved six Belorussian Jews from murder squads in 1942 and shielded another thirty-five to forty who worked under his command. He is one of more than 250 Germans and Austrians honoured for denying the gas chambers, the gallows and the machine-guns their prey. At least one of them, a devious Austrian sergeant, paid with his life. Factory managers, like Oskar Schindler, wheeled and dealed to defend their labourers. A countess smuggled runaway Jews through the sewers of Berlin. An officer's wife mothered Jewish girls working as 'Ukrainian' house-maids. A champion boxer saved two boys from a Nazi mob.

No doubt, there were others who did their 'little', but it never added up to much. Even for those who did not share the appetite of the congenital anti-Semite or the dedicated Nazi, it was easier to acquiesce. Like Adolf Eichmann, who stoked the furnace of the Final Solution, most Germans obeyed orders. Ignorance was no defence. Anyone who wanted to see, Armann testified, could see. Many had known about the concentration camps and about *Kristallnacht*, the night of shattered glass on 9–10 November 1938 when Jewish property was sacked all over the Reich. They had seen their Jewish neighbours wearing the yellow star and being taken to the railway station. 'Everybody knew the Jews weren't being shipped to paradise.'

Hugo Armann was twenty-two when he was drafted for the war. As a teenager he had joined the Hitler Youth, but soon dropped out. His parents were anti-Nazi. They had Jewish friends and business associates, who visited their home. In 1942, after Germany attacked the Soviet Union, he was posted as a sergeant-major to the Belorussian town of Baranowicze. He was in charge of issuing rail tickets to soldiers and security policemen who were going home on leave. His office was located at the railway station. Leave tickets were in great demand. Officers, he quickly found, were ready to trade favours for favours. 'I exploited my advantage to bribe people so that I could help people in need,' he confessed later. 'I used my position to obtain Jewish helpers and to supply starving people with food.'

Baranowicze's 10,000 Jews were herded into a ghetto and set to work as slave labourers. One of Armann's Jewish staff was Sara Czazkes, a nineteen-year-old girl, who worked in his unit's kitchen. He was, she remembered, 'a very noble, exceptionally good man'. In March 1942, during Purim, the carnival festival when Jews celebrate their rescue from destruction at the hands of the Persian King Ahasuerus and his evil minister, Haman, in the fifth century BC, the Gestapo and local police collaborators dragged 2,300 men from their homes, taunted, bludgeoned and shot them to death. They included the heads of the *Judenrat* (Jewish council), who had refused to co-operate with the regime. Six months later, Armann heard from one of his security police clients that there was to be a second massacre the day after Yom Kippur, the Day of Atonement. This time it was the turn of the women and children. The sergeant-major made plans to protect 'his' Jews.

'We were destined to die [Sara Czazkes recalled], but Hugo Armann rescued the entire group of Jews that worked for him. He took us out from the selection place and kept us in his house till the *shechitah* [slaughter] was over.' In this letter, written to Yad Vashem from Baltimore in 1985, Sara switched from English to Hebrew to define what happened in Baranowicze as '*shechitah*'. The word has echoes of both animal slaughter and the Czarist pogroms. The English equivalent was too vapid.

In the course of ten days, another 3,000 Jews were killed. Hundreds of victims were hastily buried that autumn in common graves, so shallow that packs of dogs dug up and devoured their corpses.

No one imagined that the second massacre would be the last. Sara continued working for Armann's unit, but, instead of going back to the ghetto at night, she and the other Jewish kitchen hands stayed in the sergeant-major's house. The third blow fell in December, when the ghetto was destroyed and a further 3,000 were killed. All but the most essential Jewish workers were ordered to return home, but Armann kept his charges in the attic for three more weeks till the 'action' was over.

It had become too dangerous for them to stay any longer. Armann contacted a Polish underground fighter, Edward Czaczia, who guided Jews escaping from the ghetto to join the partisans in the forest. Czaczia smuggled Sara to a marsh, about twelve miles out of town, which served as a way station for Jewish and other fugitives. Before transferring her to the resistance man's care, Armann gave Sara his Walther service revolver. 'He put his own life at great risk,' Sara's brother-in-law, Dr Shabtai Sternfeld, testified. 'If, God forbid, he had been caught, it would have been the end of Armann.'

Not content with saving Sara's life, Armann sought out her father, sister and brother-in-law, who worked in labour camps outside the ghetto, and eventually helped them and two other Jews to escape and join her in the forest. Sara's father, Josef, a watchmaker, lived in overcrowded barracks. Armann went secretly to see him and to discuss ways to help. 'The workers lived and slept in one room,' he recounted. 'Bunks, filled with people, reached up to the ceiling. I brought them fresh and tinned food and bread.' Hearing that Dr Sternfeld was working as camp doctor, he asked for a check-up. The medical took place in the home of an SD man. Again, Armann used the visit to discuss how he could help. He went back and forth to the camp, bringing news of Sara, which he had received from Czaczia. In November 1943, Sternfeld, his wife, Faigel, and his father-in-law escaped from the camp. 'Armann served as the go-between for us and Czaczia,' the doctor wrote. 'He was the active organizer of our escape. Czaczia brought us to a safe place.'

The dissident sergeant-major was also in touch with a group of Jewish mechanics who worked in the camp garage. They asked him for weapons. 'I took my car to the garage,' Armann wrote, 'the doors closed behind me. Under the back seat I had hidden rifles and ammunition.' With or without his assistance, at least 450 Jews are estimated to have escaped to the forest.

Hugo Armann remained in Baranowicze till mid-1944, when he was transferred to the western front. He was wounded by shrapnel in France. After the war he taught at a school in the West German town of Detter. Dr Sternfeld, who settled in Tel Aviv, sent him an annual gift box of Jaffa oranges. Before his death in May 1989, Armann ended a letter to Yad Vashem: 'Did I do much? Did I do too little? Did I do my duty?' An earlier passage in the same letter furnished the definitive answer. 'I helped human beings', he wrote, 'at a time when they were not treated like human beings.'

• • •

Anton Schmid was the Scarlet Pimpernel, or perhaps the Robin Hood, of the Vilna ghetto. He inspired legends. Survivors claimed that he spoke to them in Yiddish or Hebrew; that he had visited kibbutzim in Palestine; that he did, or did not, consort with criminals. Some said that he never died. Schmid was a Wehrmacht sergeant in charge of Jewish slave labourers. He was a man without illusions. He was proud of being an Austrian and not a German. He despised the Nazis, but did not underestimate them. On New Year's Eve 1942, he drank a discreet toast with two young Jews, Mordechai Tannenbaum and Esther Yafee. He was already smuggling Jews out of Vilna. He helped underground fighters to reach Poland and report to leaders of the Warsaw ghetto. There were stories that he pulled rank to free Jews picked up by the Lithuanian police, and that he escorted workers back to the ghetto to prevent the guards confiscating their contraband food. On days when Jews were to be rounded up, Schmid warned his workers. Tannenbaum joked that after the war he would be awarded a medal in Palestine for saving Jews. Schmid said that he would be proud to wear it.

In February, everyone living in the Vilna ghetto was issued with an identity card: white for the unskilled, yellow for those with skills the Germans could use. It was assumed that holders of yellow cards and their families would be kept alive, and that white cardholders were condemned. Only fifteen of Schmid's men were favoured with yellow. 'The yellow cards and the white cards are the same garbage,' the sergeant told them. 'One way or the other, all the Jews will be liquidated.'

For all his scepticism, Schmid resolved to move the white cardholders out of harm's way. He hid them in army trucks and drove them to Lida, which at that time was across the shifting border in Belorussia. The Jewish community of Lida was not yet penned in a ghetto. There were no round-ups, though later that year 16,000 Jews were massacred in a single operation. Shlomo Bronowski, an engineer who received one of the yellow IDs, but lost both his wife and son in Vilna, reported:

'Between two and five times a week Schmid would haul logs from the Vilna area to a place halfway to Lida. That's how he transported the Jews. In this way he managed to move about 300 Jewish families to Lida. Two of his workers, Jews who had been part of the criminal world, helped him to carry out his evacuation. They were called Berkeh der Gabbai and Smurah. They influenced Schmid, who at first offered his help with no thought for reward, to get jewellery and furs from those he was moving out. They themselves, in their role as middlemen, took a cut.'

Other survivors contended that Schmid took payment not for himself, but to feed the people he was rescuing and to entertain Germans in a position to help him. 'It was understood by all', one witness said, 'that in order to get Jews out he had to meet people and drink with them. In those days, whisky was hard to come by for love or money. We understood that the sums were needed to finance his activities. The people in the ghetto saw nothing wrong in this. Rather the opposite. Those were the terms of life in the ghetto. In any case, he was not too extortionate. Those who gave, gave. Those who didn't, didn't.' The Pimpernel could do no wrong, though Yad Vashem worried about the payments and thought twice before honouring him.

Schmid's luck ran out a few weeks later when the Nazis established a ghetto in Lida. They discovered a suspicious number of Vilna Jews and began to investigate. At first, no one would talk, but eventually the truth came out. Schmid was arrested and held in the Stefanska military prison. Under interrogation, he revealed that a Jewish tailor in one of his workshops was making him a suit. The police summoned the workers' representative, Abraham Frankel, and forced him to bring the suit. Schmid was confronted with this evidence of corruption. Frankel was never heard of again. Another sergeant, a man called

Fuchs, took over the unit. He appointed a reluctant Shlomo Bronowski in Frankel's place.

'On the morning of 2 April 1942 [Bronowski remembered], when I went into the main office to take the keys, I saw a soldier I knew who worked in the office. He was sad and quiet. When I asked him why, he replied that Schmid had been shot that morning as a traitor to the Fatherland.'

• • •

Eberhard Helmrich, a major in the German army of occupation, and his wife Donata knew that they were risking their lives. If the Gestapo discovered that they were sheltering Jews not only in Poland but also in the heart of the Reich, in Berlin itself, their four children would find themselves orphans. For a long week, they weighed the conflicting obligations, then they decided that they preferred their children to be orphans rather than the children of cowards. So Eberhard wheeled and dealed to protect nearly 300 Jewish forced labourers on the farm he managed for the Wehrmacht near the Galician town of Drohobicz. Donata brought at least five thinly disguised Jewish girls to work as 'Ukrainian' housemaids in Berlin and Hamburg. According to one witness, they also found maids' jobs for another 100 Jewish women in Poland. Eberhard forged Aryan papers for many of them in his cellar. The couple consoled themselves with the thought that, 'after we had saved two people, we'd be even with Hitler if we were caught, and with every person saved beyond that, we were ahead'.

The Helmrichs had helped Jews before the war. They sailed back and forth to England, smuggling out the valuables – and occasionally the children – of their Jewish friends. Just before *Kristallnacht* in November 1938, when the Nazis started rounding up German Jews, the Helmrichs telephoned a Jewish lawyer and his wife and told them to pack a suitcase and come to them immediately. 'They did this,' the lawyer's son, Harvey Samo, recorded, 'stayed in the Helmrich home for about ten days, and, therefore, were saved from arrest and deportation to a concentration camp.'

Despite his anti-Nazism, Eberhard joined the army and was appointed a supplies officer. In Drohobicz, his job was to feed the German troops garrisoned in the area. He established a farm, employing about 300 'healthy and fit young men and women', almost ninety per cent of whom were Jews. The harvests were excellent, the troops were fed, their commanders were satisfied. During the mass murders and deportations from Drohobicz in the autumn of 1942 and the spring and summer of 1943, Eberhard resisted repeated orders to hand over his young workers. He explained to his superiors that it would destroy the farm and he would not be able to supply food to the army. He also bribed Gestapo agents with produce from the farm. The major sometimes protected Jews who were not working for him. When the Gestapo picked up Dr Sasha Weissman, a surgeon, four times in the streets of the Drohobicz ghetto, Eberhard talked them into releasing him on each occasion. He pleaded that the doctor, whom he had provided with forged papers certifying that he was an agricultural specialist, was needed to keep the farm running. Once he hid Dr Weissman and his wife in his home for thirty-six hours when the Gestapo were hunting them. The extermination was so ruthless that of the town's 15,000 pre-war Jewish population, plus hundreds more who took shelter there before the German invasion, only 400 survivors emerged from hiding when the Red Army entered Drohobicz in August 1944.

In November 1942, Eberhard went to Berlin on leave, bringing his wife back with him for a visit. Donata had told him that domestic staff was hard to find because German women had been drafted into factories to replace men who had gone to the army. In Drohobicz, Eberhard himself employed a sixteen-year-old Jewish girl, Susi Almann, as his housekeeper. Susi's father, Wilhelm, was a Viennese businessman who had fled to Galicia when Hitler took over Austria in 1938. Eberhard had recruited him as head of his Jewish farm workers. Susi found conditions in the Helmrich household tolerable enough:

'Eberhard Helmrich had a nice house there. He entertained a lot of Germans. He had a Ukrainian cook who hated the Germans and who always spat in the food before I took it to the table. Once he was entertaining a couple of Nazis. One of them said, "It's time all the Jews were liquidated." Helmrich was worried that I would react. He said to the Nazi, "That's not the kind of thing to talk about at the table." '

Susi, now Susi Bezalel, living in the Tel Aviv suburb of Ramat

Chen, became the first of the Jewish girls Frau Helmrich took back to help solve the servant problem:

'This was the time when they started to kill people, even on the farm, cripples, old people. It was in the air that youngsters would be killed. The Helmrichs arranged with my parents that when the actions started, they would come and take me and my younger sister, Hansi, to Berlin. My father procured for me a false birth certificate. These were papers bought from a living person in case the Germans checked the church register. I bought a Ukrainian blouse, then said goodbye to my mother and father.

'I went by train with Donata Helmrich. We didn't ride in the same compartment. She went first class. I knew some Ukrainian from my schooldays under Russian occupation. I was excited. I was practising the catechism in Ukrainian. I had a whole story prepared to explain how I spoke such good German. I would tell anyone who asked that I had German foster parents. In Berlin we had to be processed in transit camps. I was very frightened. I got a permit to work in a household. They checked us for lice. We had to strip and walk with hands on head. Our clothes were deloused. Then we got our identity cards.'

At first, Donata took Susi as her own maid, but was worried that the girl would be spotted. The Helmrichs had a reputation for being friendly to Jews. Susi herself not only looked distinctly Semitic, but was also quick to react to injustice. 'It is one thing to dispatch a young girl into a faraway country,' Susi marvelled afterwards, 'and another thing to take her into your own home, into your family, a family with four children. How did Frau Helmrich know that I, or the girls she received afterwards, would not give ourselves away in a fit of anger, fear, surprise, thus implicating her and her kids?' Donata soon placed Susi with a retired couple, who lived in an elegant villa in Potsdam, without, of course, telling them that their new maid was a Jewess. Luckily, there were no real Ukrainian maids in the neighbourhood who might have unmasked her.

'My couple were very proper [Susi told me] from Hanover. He had been a big shot in the Nestlé chocolate company. Because of their age, they qualified for a maid. When they were evacuated from Berlin, the labour bureau assigned me to the wife of an admiral. There were pictures everywhere of the admiral with

Hitler. The wife liked me a lot. My luck was that the bombing of Berlin started. I spent a lot of time in the shelter. The couple were away, but they came every few weeks to see everything was all right. They brought lots of washing. I washed on a board. Sometimes I was alone in the villa. Sometimes the Government sent people who were bombed out. So the admiral and his wife were very happy to have me keeping an eye on things.'

Later, Eberhard Helmrich sent Susi's sister, Hansi, to Donata in Berlin escorted by his secretary. The Helmrichs placed three more girls in Hamburg. All five came through the war. Two live now in Israel, one in the United States, one in Germany, and Susi's sister in Australia. Throughout the two years she worked as a Ukrainian maid, Susi kept in touch with Donata, visiting her occasionally, telephoning more often. Frau Helmrich became her unofficial adoptive mother. Susi called her 'Mammy'. She often visited her sister, who worked in a villa five minutes' walk from the Helmrichs' home. Hansi's employers, an eminent scientist and his wife, knew that she was Jewish.

Eberhard did not visit Susi until the end of the war. Even then, he judged it kinder not to tell her that her father had poisoned himself rather than fall into the hands of the Nazis and that her mother, working as a maid in Poland, had been betrayed and killed. The Helmrichs survived, but not their marriage. Eberhard divorced Donata and married one of the Jewish girls he had saved from the Gestapo. They moved to New York. Donata served as private secretary to Konrad Adenauer, the federal Chancellor who initiated Germany's reconciliation with Israel and the Jewish people. She retired to a fisherman's thatched cottage on the North Sea island of Sylt.

Israel honoured Eberhard Helmrich in 1965 and Donata twenty-one years later. Frau Helmrich died before she could receive the Yad Vashem award. Their daughter, Cornelia Schmalz-Jacobsen, a Free Democratic member of the Berlin senate, planted a tree in her memory. 'The war wrought many changes,' she reflected. 'My father is buried in New York and my mother on the island of Sylt. Here on the Avenue of the Righteous among the Nations they are reunited.'

• ● •

Like Eberhard Helmrich, Roman Erich Petsche was an officer in the Wehrmacht. Like Anton Schmid, he was an Austrian. Like both of them, he refused to disqualify the Jews from the human race. As the Final Solution closed in, he felt compassion for specific Jews, people he saw every day, and he did something about it. If he had been caught, that something would have brought him before a firing squad, as it brought Anton Schmid in another corner of the European nightmare.

Petsche was one of a batch of officers billeted in the home of the prosperous Csernyei family after the Nazis marched into the Danubian city of Novi Sad in 1944. The Jewish owners were left only two small rooms for themselves. Among those living there were the wife and five-year-old twin daughters of a leading lawyer, Gyorgy Tibor, who had been captured a few months earlier trying to escape across the Yugoslav–Hungarian border and was never heard of again. Despite the cramped conditions, the Tibors had moved in with their Csernyei kinsfolk. Petsche, a Viennese artist before and after the war, befriended them, helping them with food and other necessities. On 24 March 1944, the Nazis ordered the 4,000 or so Jews who had survived the earlier occupation by Hitler's Hungarian allies to report to the synagogue the next day for transportation to Auschwitz. When Petsche returned to his lodgings that evening and heard the news, he resolved to cheat the extermination machine.

He told Vera Tibor to dress her twins, Miriam and Hava. Within minutes, the little girls were ready and Petsche drove them to the railway station along with a cleaning woman he knew. He claimed that the woman was his wife and the twins his own daughters. That night the train took them all across the Hungarian border to Budapest, where Petsche delivered Miriam and Hava to an aunt. The Hungarian capital itself was no longer a safe haven, so the aunt handed them on to a Roman Catholic convent outside the city, where the mother superior, a Jewish convert, kept them until the liberation.

The same night, Petsche went straight back to Novi Sad and set about helping the twins' mother and other relatives. There was little he could do at short notice. He gave them food for the journey and advised them to jump off the train taking them through his native Austria to Auschwitz. He gave them his wife's address in

Vienna and begged them to let her shelter them. In fact, no one from Novi Sad jumped out. The Germans had intimidated them with threats that if a single passenger was missing when the train arrived at the camp, they would slaughter everyone immediately. Only the twins' sick old grandmother stayed behind in Novi Sad. Petsche installed her in a local hospital, where he visited her every day until she died.

In all, seven members of the Tibor and Csernyei families were deported from Novi Sad to Auschwitz. Only one, the twins' aunt, Olga Csernyei, came back from the death camp. Olga, Miriam and Hava settled in Israel. Miriam (now Mrs Ascher) lives in Ramat Gan, near Tel Aviv, and Hava (Mrs Szyk) in Lehavot Haviva, a modest kibbutz in the plain of Sharon, where she runs the library and cultural programmes. The twins exchanged Christmas and birthday cards with Roman Erich Petsche into the 1990s, though they never again met their Wehrmacht saviour after the night he posed as their father on the train to Budapest.

• • •

You did not have to be a saint to be righteous. Oskar Schindler, a Sudeten German industrialist who saved 1,200 of his Jewish workers from the shadow of Auschwitz, drank and slept around. Before going into business, he served in German counter-espionage. After the war, he was hauled back twice from the verge of bankruptcy, in Argentina and in Germany. Whenever he had money, he spent it. In his favourite bars, it would be drinks all round. If friends invited him for dinner, he would send his hostess 100 roses. MGM bought his story for $50,000 in the 1960s. Barely a week after he had received an advance of $20,000, half of it had gone. Moshe Bejski, a young Polish Jewish draughtsman in Schindler's enamelware factory who became an Israeli supreme court judge, summed him up, prosecution and defence:

'Schindler was a drunkard, Schindler was a womanizer. His relations with his wife were rather bad. Each time he had not one but several girlfriends. After the war, he was quite unable to run a normal business. During the war, as long as he could produce kitchenware and sell it on the black market and make a lot of money, he could do it. But he was unable to work normally, to calculate normally, to hold down a normal job, even in Germany.

A group of survivors in Israel raised some money for him when he was hard up. If we sent $3,000–$4,000, he spent it within two or three weeks, then 'phoned to say he didn't have a penny. He spent money quicker than we could raise it.

'So, I am aware of who Schindler was, but without Schindler most of those 1,200 Jews would not have remained alive, certainly not as a group. You had to take him as he was. Schindler was a very complex person. Schindler was a good human being. He was against evil. He acted spontaneously. He was adventurous, someone who took risks, but I'm not sure he enjoyed taking them. He did things because people asked him to do them. He loved children. He saw all the children and grandchildren of those he had rescued as his own family. He was very, very sensitive. If Schindler had been a normal man, he would not have done what he did. Everything he did put him in danger. He could have done much less, and still qualified as one of the righteous.

'One day in the late 1960s I asked Schindler why he did all this. His answer was very simple: "I knew the people who worked for me. When you know people, you have to behave towards them like human beings. If I'm walking in the street and I see a dog in danger of being crushed by a car, wouldn't I try to help him?" That was Schindler.'

Moshe Bejski must be the only supreme court judge in the world to have started his working life as a master forger. Schindler employed him not only to draw blueprints, but also to counterfeit official documents. He had learned his skill in the Cracow ghetto, forging Aryan papers for Jewish girls, who used them to seek work in Germany. In his bungalow near Tel Aviv University, Bejski shows visitors the draughtsman's instruments Schindler gave him – and the rubber stamp, complete with German eagle, which he carved with a razor blade in Schindler's factory.

Soon after the Nazi invasion of Poland, Schindler, then aged thirty-one, went to Cracow and bought a confiscated Jewish factory from its German 'trustees'. One of the first people he met in Cracow was a scholarly Jewish accountant, Isaac Stern, who was to serve as his faithful lieutenant for the next five years. When they introduced themselves, Schindler held out his hand. Stern declined to take it. When Schindler asked why, he explained that he was a Jew and it was forbidden for a Jew to shake a German's hand. Schindler answered with a Teutonic expletive: *'Scheisse'* ('shit'). Stern could tell from the start that this was no ordinary German.

The twenty-two-year-old Bejski first heard of Schindler in 1943, a few months after being transferred from the ghetto to the notoriously harsh Plaszow labour camp nearby. A squad of Jews used to go every day from the ghetto to work in Schindler's plant. When the ghetto was liquidated in March, the workforce and a few thousand other Jews were lodged in Plaszow. The workers continued to go to Schindler every morning under armed escort and came back every evening. The industrialist soon persuaded the authorities to let him establish a branch of the camp in his factory. A few dozen of his workers moved into barracks he built for them. According to Bejski, conditions there were far superior to those in the camp:

'There was no killing whatsoever in the Schindler camp. In Plaszow hardly a day passed when there were no killings. Every German could kill at will. Schindler's people didn't work as hard as we worked in Plaszow. We worked fourteen to eighteen hours a day. Schindler provided supplementary food for his workers. An extra half a loaf of bread was very important in those times. Schindler was supposed to be making kitchenware for the army, but he sold part of it on the black market. I never saw Schindler at this time, but it was much desired to be transferred to the Schindler camp.'

During the course of 1943 and 1944, Schindler expanded his workforce from a couple of dozen to 700. A party of SS officers on a tour of inspection accused a prisoner of sabotage because he was slow pushing a wheelbarrow across the factory yard. They sent him to Plaszow to be shot. As soon as Schindler heard about it, he rushed to the camp and 'bought' the man's life for a bottle of vodka. Another time, two Gestapo men came to his office and demanded that he hand over a family of five who had bought forged Polish identity papers. 'Three hours after they walked in,' Schindler told the writer Kurt Grossman, 'two drunken Gestapo men reeled out of my office without their prisoners and without the incriminating documents they had demanded.' At the request of Isaac Stern, Schindler went unhesitatingly to Budapest on a secret mission to meet Rudolf Kastner and other officials of the

Jewish rescue committee. He reported on conditions in Plaszow and Cracow and brought back a large sum of money to be distributed among Jewish leaders in the labour camp. Bejski, who worked in the registration office and had relative freedom of movement, helped Stern to deliver it.

Bejski stayed in Plaszow until October 1944. With the Russians advancing westwards, the Germans started liquidating the camp that summer, shipping the prisoners back to an ominous fate in the Reich. The population was soon reduced from about 25,000 or 30,000 to 10,000. As early as August, the Jews knew that this was the end of Plaszow. Between 2,000 and 4,000 Jews, slaughtered in the Cracow ghetto in March 1943, had been buried in mass graves at Plaszow. They were people too young, too old or too sick to travel. Seventeen months later, as the Russians advanced through Poland, the graves were reopened and the bodies were burned – after the Jews' gold teeth were removed. The camp inmates could smell the burning remains for a full month. The Germans were destroying the evidence of their atrocity. Other Jews were sent to Auschwitz, not far away.

Resourceful as ever, Schindler obtained permission to move the enamelware factory to his home town in Sudetenland – the slice of Czechoslovakia surrendered to Germany by Britain and France under the Munich agreement of 1938 – and to increase his workforce by about 400. He also won a contract to manufacture shells as well as kitchenware. Competition to get on to Schindler's list was intense. Everyone knew that there was a better chance of staying alive with the maverick businessman than in the concentration camps.

'Everyone who could find a way to get on the list did his best [Bejski recalled]. There were some wealthy people who still had diamonds hidden away. About a dozen of them bribed a Jewish alderman who was drawing up the list. People tried to approach the alderman through his friends. Some tried to go straight to Schindler. People working for Schindler tried to get him to include their relatives from the camp. Schindler asked that some prominent Jewish leaders should be put on the list. He also took about seventy workers from a factory making army uniforms. Fortunately for me, I came on the list as a technical designer because I had some knowledge of technical drawing.'

Bejski and his two brothers were among about 800 'Schindler Jews' dispatched west by cattle truck to Gross Rosen concentration camp in Upper Silesia:

'It was about 100 kilometres, but it took two or three days to get there. We had to wait in different railway stations for hours. We got food for one day, which we ate on the first day. We arrived at Gross Rosen late in the afternoon. We saw the chimneys of the crematoria burning. We weren't so sure we were going to Schindler. We were kept outside all night for a very exact body search, even internal. We were naked all night on a very cold late October night. I got my clothes at eleven o'clock the next morning.

'The first sign that we were going to Schindler was that they put us in a special barracks. The conditions were so cramped that nobody could sleep for a week. Then one day we were transferred to the wagons, 80–100 in one cattle truck. What interested us was which direction the train would take. We went south towards Czechoslovakia. It took another two or three days with only 150 grammes of bread each. We stopped a long time at every station. There were a lot of troop movements. Then we came to Brünnlitz, near Schindler's birthplace, Zwittau. Schindler was not there, the factory equipment had not yet arrived, but we were put in three big rooms on the upper floor. We slept on the floor on loose straw. Later Schindler provided three-tiered bunks with straw in bags. What was important was that we were in Schindler's factory.'

The 800 men arrived, but 300 women who were supposed to complete the list were sent to Auschwitz. Most of them were mothers, wives and sisters of the Schindler men, who begged Isaac Stern to intercede. Schindler responded immediately. He sent his secretary, a German woman, to Auschwitz with a bag of diamonds to bribe the authorities. After a couple of weeks, the 300 women arrived in Brünnlitz. The only one left behind was Stern's elderly mother, who died in Auschwitz. It is the only recorded instance where so many women came out of the camp and survived. Again, Schindler did more than simple decency required. He could have shrugged and said, 'There's nothing I can do. It's too risky to try and get them out.' Instead, he followed his instincts – and got away with it.

On another occasion, he heard that a train had arrived at Zwittau with two wagons packed with Jews from Golleschau, a branch of

Auschwitz. In the chaos of that last winter of the war, they had been travelling for two weeks without food, water or destination. Schindler managed to get hold of the bill of lading and wrote in 'Zwittau' as the destination. He took a welding crew from his factory and opened the wagons. About 100 emaciated Jews were still alive, but seventeen had frozen to death. Schindler's factory was part of an SS camp. The commandant ordered that the bodies be burned. Schindler went to the local council and arranged for the Jews to be buried according to their own tradition in a corner of the cemetery. He persuaded the SS chief to allow him to take a *minyan* of ten prisoners, including one who was a rabbi, to bury them. Schindler's long-suffering wife, Emilia, nursed the 100 Golleschau survivors and fed them with porridge. She travelled 200 miles to trade two suitcases of vodka – one of the staples of Schindler's black-market commerce – for medicines for them. The survivors weighed barely seventy pounds each. The SS commandant ordered that these walking skeletons be made to work. Schindler knew that it was impossible for most of them to do so, but for the rest of the war he paid Berlin the same five marks a day tax for them as he paid for every other slave labourer.

Schindler showed his compassion on a smaller scale too. As he walked past Bejski's drawing table he would light a cigarette, put down the packet while he stopped to inspect his work, then 'forget' to pick it up again. Four cigarettes would buy the best part of a loaf of bread. A man whose glasses were broken could not see without them. Schindler went to town and bought him a new pair. One of the women prisoners became pregnant. If the SS commandant had found out, the woman would have been sent straight to the gas chambers. Schindler procured surgical instruments and arranged for one of his Jewish workers, a doctor, to perform an abortion. The woman survived the war and now lives in Israel. Another young woman was dying of tuberculosis. She craved for an apple. It was mid-winter in a forced labour camp, but somehow Schindler found her one. Some of the prisoners had hidden their children with Polish families. Schindler smuggled letters to Cracow and brought back news of the youngsters.

In the factory, he shielded his original 1,100 Jews. They were chronically undernourished, even though Schindler supplemented their starvation rations. Production was often lethargic.

THE FEW WHO DISOBEYED

Schindler barred the brutal SS guards from his plant. The daily roll call took place in the yard outside. When he himself entered, no one concealed the fact that they were not working hard enough. He did nothing about it.

Not content with bringing 'his' Jews to the Sudetenland and protecting them from the Nazis, Schindler continued to buy and sell on the Polish black market – and to bribe German officers and Nazi officials wholesale. That was how the future Judge Bejski became his master forger. Schindler needed permits to transport food and other commodities from Cracow to Germany and Czechoslovakia. Isaac Stern knew of Bejski's record of forging Aryan papers in the ghetto. Schindler acquired one genuine permit and set him to work copying it, seal and all. Bejski is still puzzled at the extra risk his boss was taking. Every new adventure increased the prospect of detection. Schindler was arrested twice, but told Bejski later that he had bribed his way out. It did not stop him going on to the last.

By March 1945, it was clear to everyone in Brünnlitz that the war was won and lost. Two of the Jewish workers were radio technicians. Schindler used to give them radios to repair for the German staff. The technicians took the chance to listen to the BBC's Polish service. Once, Schindler 'forgot' to collect a set for a whole week. The prisoners plotted the Allied advances on an improvised map, but they knew that it was too early to celebrate. If the SS followed their usual pattern, the Jews would be force-marched into the Reich, with every possibility that they would die along the way. At the same time, Schindler was worried about what would happen to him, as a German capitalist with dubious connections, if he fell into Soviet hands. His response to the dual dilemma was as audacious as ever.

Schindler told the Jews that he had a clandestine stock of rifles, revolvers and hand-grenades concealed in a store-room next to his flat. He gave the key to Bejski's younger brother, Uri, who worked for him as a domestic servant. If the SS tried to take the Jews out, he said, they should revolt and make a break for it. A Jew who had been an officer in the Polish army taught fifteen prisoners one by one how to use the weapons. 'Till 8 May,' Moshe Bejski said, 'we were not sure if the commandant would take us on a death march.' During the afternoon of VE (Victory in Europe) Day, the weapons were distributed among the fifteen marksmen, who deployed themselves around the factory, but that night the SS withdrew on their own.

Schindler had promised that he would not abandon his charges until the last SS man had pulled out. He kept his word. But five minutes after the Nazi evacuation, he headed west in a truck, driven by a Jewish volunteer, Richard Rechen, who now lives in Haifa. The Jews debated what to give their saviour in return. They gave him letters in German and Hebrew, addressed to any Jewish official he might encounter, testifying that he had saved their lives and deserved to be helped. It did not seem enough, but they had nothing else. Then a Jew by the name of Jeret offered a set of gold teeth, which were immediately extracted. Another prisoner, a jeweller called Licht, made them into a ring inscribed to Schindler with thanks. Before leaving, Schindler broke open his black-market storehouse and distributed a bottle of vodka, 200 cigarettes and a suit-length of navy blue cloth to each prisoner to help them on their way to freedom.

Schindler and Rechen eluded the Russians and reached Paris, where the fugitive industrialist was rewarded by the American Jewish Joint Distribution Committee with $15,000 to buy his ill-fated farm in Argentina. When Schindler paid the first of seventeen visits to Israel in 1961, some 220 exuberant survivors turned out to greet him. What, one of them asked, had happened to the gold ring? 'Schnapps,' he shrugged. It had gone to buy booze. That, as Judge Bejski said, was Oskar Schindler. You had to take him as you found him. He died of an over-extended liver in Hanover in October 1974 and was buried on Mount Zion in Jerusalem in the presence of more than 400 Schindler survivors and their families. The Catholic cemetery had never seen so many grieving Jews.

· · ·

If you believed Nazi propaganda, Max Schmeling was the last German you would have expected to rescue two Jewish teenagers from an Aryan mob. Or to have had Jewish friends. Schmeling won the world heavyweight boxing title in 1930. Six years later, he created a sensation by knocking out the rising black American, Joe Louis, in the twelfth round. It was the 'Brown Bomber's' first defeat. Although he was not yet world champion, Louis had already thrashed the former title-holders, Primo Carnera and Max Baer. The Nazi press trumpeted Schmeling's triumph as 'a victory for the white race'. Schmeling was projected as the Teutonic myth made flesh and muscle, the ultimate Nazi hero, even though Louis took his revenge with a first-round knockout in 1938 and went on to hold the world title undefeated for another eleven years.

David Lewin, a flamboyant Jewish businessman with a passion for sport and the cabaret world of the sickly Weimar Republic, met Schmeling in the early 1930s. Like many German Jews, he was more German than Jewish. He had a box at the opera, the best seats at the motor races and the fights. Lewin owned a flourishing hotel and restaurant business in Potsdam, just outside Berlin. Schmeling trained there for his big bouts. The two men shared a favourite night spot, the Zigeunerkeller, the Gypsy Cellar, where they drank and sang together.

By 1938, with Hitler entrenched and anti-Semitism rising to a crescendo, Lewin could read the signs. He moved his family to Berlin and prepared to emigrate. On the night of 9 November, *Kristallnacht*, he turned to his fighter friend. Schmeling, by then aged thirty-three, was in the capital on a business trip. Lewin asked him to look after his two sons, Heinz and Werner, aged fourteen and fifteen respectively. Schmeling took them to his room in the Excelsior Hotel on Alexanderplatz and kept them there for three days. He told the front desk that he was ill and must not be disturbed. On the 12th, when the riots abated, Schmeling drove them to his home in his Mercedes convertible. After waiting another two days, he delivered them to their father. Soon afterwards the family sailed for Shanghai, where David went into hotel management. They moved to the United States in 1946.

Schmeling's act of shelter remained secret for fifty-one years until Heinz Lewin, by then Henri and president of the Sands Hotel in Las Vegas, organized a gala dinner in a style that his father would have relished. He assembled '800 of the most famous names in boxing' to honour the eighty-four-year-old bruiser, seated next to the reigning heavyweight champion, Mike Tyson. 'I'm going to tell you what kind of a champion Max Schmeling is,' Lewin announced. 'He risked everything for us. If we had been found in his room, I would not be here this evening and neither would Max.'

Lewin explained afterwards that his father had already bought the tickets to Shanghai. If the family had been picked up on *Kristallnacht*, they might well have missed their last chance to get out. Uncles, aunts and cousins were arrested about that time and were never heard of again.

'There is no question [he told me] that Schmeling would have been in great danger if we had been discovered. The Nazis could not afford to let a national hero be a Jew lover. He would have disgraced the Führer. He also took a tremendous risk by driving us in his own car. He could have put us in a taxi. But we were his friends, and he would do anything for us. It was the only time my father asked him for anything.'

Lewin had kept the story secret at Schmeling's request. Even when the ex-champion agreed to attend the Las Vegas dinner, he asked his host not to glorify him. 'He told me that what he had done for me and my brother was doing the duty of a man,' added Lewin, who explained that he had gone public because 'Max is eighty-four, though in excellent shape, and I'm sixty-five, and I wasn't sure how much longer both of us would last.'

Although he was exploited by Joseph Goebbels's propaganda machine, Schmeling was never a Nazi. He had other Jewish friends besides David Lewin. He served in the paratroops during the war, and built a prosperous business career afterwards as the Coca-Cola distributor for West Germany. Henri Lewin kept his distance, though he inherited his father's love of boxing and high life. In 1980, Schmeling contacted him after reading in a German newspaper that he was promoting a world title fight in the Las Vegas Hilton, where he was then vice-president. Henri took up the friendship where David had left off. In 1981, when Joe Louis died still trying to clear his debts to the Internal Revenue Service, Schmeling asked Lewin to represent him at the funeral and sent him a large sum of money for Louis's widow. That, too, went unpublicized until 1989.

• • •

Countess Maria Helena Françoise Isabel von Maltzan, the rebellious daughter of an aristocratic German-Swedish house, was once asked how she could live through the war with Death sitting on her shoulder. 'You can only do so if you don't see him,' she replied. 'If I had had a second of fear, I would have been dead. But at the moment something looks dangerous, I work out what I can do. And even in the worst times, I have always seen the comic in things.'

The Countess was born in 1909 and grew up in a castle on the 18,000-acre von Maltzan estate in Silesia. When Hitler came to power, most of her family joined the National Socialist Party. Her mother hated Jews. Her brother, a fervent Nazi, would later cut her off from her inheritance. A sister was married to Field-Marshal Walter von Reichenau, one of the first senior officers to embrace Nazism. Maria studied science at the universities of Breslau and Munich, where she became active in the anti-Nazi resistance, while retaining her social connections with the German establishment. During the war, she trained as a veterinarian.

In Berlin in 1939, she met and fell in love with Hans Hirschel, the Jewish editor of an avant-garde literary magazine. Three years later, fearing that he would be deported to a concentration camp, she invited him to move into her three-roomed flat in Detmolder Strasse, where she hid him for the rest of the war in a large mahogany daybed, which could be opened to store bedding. The flat was under frequent surveillance by the Gestapo. Hirschel had no money and no ration coupons. She shared her food with him and worked at two jobs – to keep them both and to fund her wider rescue activities. According to Hirschel, her health was ruined and she almost suffered a nervous collapse because of the constant tension. When she found herself pregnant, she persuaded a Swedish homosexual friend to pose as the father. A son, born prematurely in September 1942, died in a Berlin hospital when an air raid cut the power supply to his incubator.

Hirschel was not the only Jew to find sanctuary in the Countess's home. She is estimated to have hidden at least sixty there at various times between 1939 and 1945. One of them, Wolfgang Hammerschmidt, a young half-Jew who later worked for ZDF television, had escaped from the Gestapo. He was suffering from pneumonia. He stayed with her from 12 March 1945 until the end of April. She nursed him and made sure that he had food at a time when it was almost impossible to find any in the beleaguered capital. A 1986 feature film, *Forbidden*, suggested that she joined the resistance because of her romance with Hirschel. She hotly denied it. 'I saved Jews', she told Janet Watts of the *Observer*, 'long before I fell in love with a Jew. I had read *Mein Kampf*. You had to be an idiot if you didn't know what would happen. I knew that murders were going on, horrible things were happening, and I would have done anything against it.'

In collaboration with the Swedish Protestant church, whose rescue work is chronicled in chapter 4, she also helped to smuggle dozens of Jews out of Germany. Pastor Erik Myrgren remembered her as the 'Lion of Berlin':

'She had a strong temperament, knew judo, swam and rode a horse like a man, or even better. She knew how to handle a pistol if necessary. At the same time she was a woman through and through, charming, elegant and very attractive. She enjoyed dealing with party functionaries, generals and brilliantined SS officers. But endless nights she changed her identity and became Maria Müller. Her activities then were incredible. Her love for Hans Hirschel was genuine love, but it was also an expression of her burning hatred against the Nazis. Sometimes she left Hans and was away for days planning means of escape and acts of resistance. The church bought Jews their freedom. She smuggled them out of Berlin through the city sewage system.'

One of her last missions was to guide a party of Jewish fugitives through the woods to a railway line. The crew of a train carrying a load of furniture for home-bound Swedish diplomats had been bribed to make an unscheduled halt. Other resistance people were waiting in the dark to prise open the crates, so that the Jews could be hidden inside. Maria delivered her charges and left. On the way back, she was detected by a Gestapo patrol with searchlights and tracker dogs. To put them off the scent, the Countess forded a stream, smeared herself with manure from a farm tip and swam across a pond. For a day and a half, cold, wet and hungry, she hid in the undergrowth waiting for a chance to make a dash for it without giving herself away. It came when air-raid sirens sounded and her pursuers took cover. As she slipped out of the woods, she saw people fighting desperately to put out a fire in a bombed factory. She joined them in their efforts, and then made her way back to town with a perfect explanation for her bedraggled state. As soon as she reached the Swedish church, Pastor Myrgren reported, she passed out.

Two Gestapo men once came to search her flat. They ordered her to open the mahogany daybed where Hans was hiding. She refused, claiming that it did not open. When they persisted, she suggested that they fired into it with their revolvers, but only after they had signed a chit promising to pay for the damage if there was nobody there. The Gestapo men thought better of it. On another occasion, when she was taken for questioning to Gestapo head-quarters, she asked the officer in charge to telephone a Nazi minister and explain why she would be late for a lunch date. It was easier to let her go. She once arrived home late at night with a bullet wound in her neck. Hirschel was horrified and asked how it had happened. She replied curtly that he must never ask questions like that.

Maria von Maltzan and Hans Hirschel married soon after the Russians took Berlin, but divorced about a year later. They remarried in 1972, three years before Hans died. When Yad Vashem asked her in 1986 to spell out her anti-Nazi activities, she wrote back: 'I know why I did what I did, and so did – I am sure – those who came to me for help. Like them, I do not cherish happy memories of those times. I can only express my sincere hope that never again may there be such hatred, such violence and such inhumanity between any human beings!'

Epilogue

Whys and Wherefores

'Please don't make too much fuss. Don't paint me as a great hero.' Everyone who has talked to rescuers has encountered the same response. 'I did my duty,' they say. 'It was the natural/humane/Christian thing to do. People were in danger. They needed help. So I helped them.' Many add that the fact that the supplicants were Jews was incidental. 'It didn't matter to us that she was Jewish,' said one of the British prisoners of war who sheltered a girl escaping from a death march. 'She was just a human being.' But the grim truth is that in Hitler's Europe to treat a Jew, any Jew, as a human being was in itself an act of heroism. 'I helped human beings', wrote the German sergeant-major, Hugo Armann, 'at a time when they were not treated like human beings.' That is the one common factor.

If rescue was so natural, why did so many millions of decent, patriotic, church-going Europeans look the other way (or worse)? The simplest answer is fear, the instinct of self-preservation. War and occupation put them and their families in imminent danger. However high our principles, none of us can be sure that we would not make the same choice. Keep out of trouble. Look after your own. But the uncertainties of total war worked in the opposite direction too. Safety was an illusion. Life was cheap. Partisans were fighting and dying. 'What had I to fear?' asked Erik Myrgren, the Swedish pastor in Berlin. 'Death was always close. The bombs were falling day and night. To take an additional risk meant so little. But for some people it was a matter of survival.' Nazi justice was rough and capricious. There was no appeal against a man with a gun who decided to shoot you, however trivial his pretext. 'In those days one looked differently at life,' a Polish rescuer told the

American author, Nechama Tec. 'Life was worthless. One could simply pass in the street and for taking out one's hand from the pocket too slowly one could be killed. I saw something like this happen. A man was shot because to an order to take his hands out of his pockets he acted too late.'

For many, however, self-protection was reinforced by a tendency to conform. The Nazis, their allies and collaborators created a climate in which it was legitimate to slaughter Jews. It demanded no great effort, bore no immediate risk, to go with the trend, to acquiesce if not to participate in the killing. You might even win merit and rewards. This tendency was most pronounced in societies where Jews were perceived as outsiders, alien intruders, an affront to national aspirations, economic competitors. It is no coincidence that the countries with the biggest concentration of unassimilated Jews – people who dressed differently, spoke a different language, worshipped differently, had links and loyalties beyond the national borders – were the countries where local auxiliaries co-operated with the greatest relish. Soviet archives opened to Western researchers during the Gorbachev honeymoon document the bloodthirsty enthusiasm with which Lithuanian, Latvian and Ukrainian police massacred, pillaged and looted. Nazism, with its cult of blood, steel and Aryan supremacy, sanctioned and channelled the impulse to destroy. In Poland, which had 3,300,000 Jews before the war, even elements of the resistance hesitated to work with the Jewish underground.

Conversely, the readiness to protect Jews, regardless of risk, was most pronounced in societies where they were a small minority, integrated into the fabric of the nation. Countries whose identity was unchallenged, where Jews posed no threat, cultural, political or economic. Denmark, with its high rate not only of assimilation but also of intermarriage, was the supreme example. The ancient Jewish communities of Italy were part of the landscape. Bulgaria, with its 50,000 Sephardim, was a rare East European state with no tradition of anti-Semitism. These were the countries where Nazism had least appeal – and where indigenous leaders could set an alternative norm. King Christian could defy the Germans with his talk of 'our Jewish fellow citizens'. In Italy, Bishop Nicolini could turn Assisi into a sanctuary. In Greece, Archbishop Damaskinos could preach that 'all Greek citizens must enjoy the same treatment from the occupation authorities, regardless of race and religion'. In France, the Vichy regime protected native Jews while abandoning refugees to its German patron. It is no accident that Holland, with its spirit of tolerance, tops the Yad Vashem table of the righteous. Even in countries with a legacy of anti-Semitism, some resistance movements offered an alternative model of behaviour. Whole books have been written about Polish rescuers, a minority but not an insignificant one. They did not operate in a vacuum.

In the end, however, a decision to act was taken individually and often on the spur of the moment. In most cases, the initial approach came from the Jew in need, who might be an acquaintance or a total stranger. Given the circumstances, there was seldom time for deliberation or to go home and discuss it with the family. You had to say 'Yes' or 'No'. One study found seventy per cent of rescuers reaching a decision within minutes and eighty per cent deciding without consulting anyone. Some believed that they were assuming a short-term commitment. They would provide a hiding-place overnight, or until the supplicant found somewhere permanent. Often this grew into weeks or months. The more the rescuer recognized 'his' Jew as a specific person, with fears and foibles, tastes and talents, the less likely he was to move him on.

What motivated those who agreed to help? In the past decade social scientists have sought an answer through the tools of their trade, interviews and questionnaires. They agree that altruism was not something born in the flicker of an eyelid. The instincts of empathy and compassion were rooted in personal history. The disposition to say 'Yes' was already there in the rescuer's character and way of life. But beyond that the research can only point to patterns of probable behaviour.

In *When Light Pierced the Darkness*, her in-depth study of Polish rescuers, Nechama Tec identifies six common traits: 1. individuality or separateness; 2. independence or self-reliance to act in accordance with personal convictions, regardless of how these are viewed by others; 3. broad and long-lasting commitment to stand up for the helpless and needy; 4. the tendency to perceive aid to Jews in a matter-of-fact unassuming way; 5. an unpremeditated, unplanned beginning of Jewish rescue; and 6. universalistic perceptions of Jews that defined them as helpless beings and as totally dependent on the protection of others. Tec concludes:

No matter what the source, these values seem to have become ingrained in the individual. All experienced them as powerful and compelling guides to personal conduct. In addition, such imperatives appear to have been incorporated into the moral makeup of these individuals well before the war. In case after case, there is a long history of giving aid to those in need.

Another researcher, Eva Fogelman, argued in her paper to a 1990 conference on moral courage during the Holocaust:

Ultimately it was childrearing, not social circumstances, that proved most significant. What kind of values were most often taught in the homes of those who became rescuers? Above all, it was a tolerance for differences among people. . . . If we instruct our children to value all life, empathize with people in distress, and tolerate differences among people, we could create a society in which an Auschwitz would be unthinkable.

Samuel and Pearl Oliner, who interviewed 700 rescuers, bystanders and survivors in the most ambitious investigation to date, *The Altruistic Personality*, come to a similar verdict:

Words and phrases characterizing care – the need to be helpful, hospitable, concerned and loving – were voiced significantly more often by rescuers as they recalled the values they learned from their parents or other most influential person. Generosity and expansiveness, rather than fairness and reciprocity, were significantly more important to rescuers' than to non-rescuers' parents. . . . Equally important, rescuers were significantly more inclusive in noting the groups to whom they felt ethical obligations.

The suffering of a stranger, the Oliners found, was as much the rescuers' responsibility as that of a friend. 'Care', they write, 'was not a spectator sport. It compelled action. It meant assuming personal responsibility, not because others required it, but because failure to act meant acquiescence in the consequences.'

Such patterns are important, but there is no key, no sufficient and necessary condition for moral courage. The Oliners' respondents with caring parents represented forty-four per cent of the rescuers they interviewed, double the proportion among those who could have saved Jews but did not. That still leaves fifty-six per cent of rescuers who did not mention caring parents. For every case that confirms a particular hypothesis, another can be found that challenges it.

Family upbringing? Yes, but what about Countess Maria von Maltzan, whose mother, brother and sister were Nazis? Liberal politics? Yes, but what about Giorgio Perlasca, who was a dedicated Fascist? Christian charity? Yes, but what about all those God-fearing Christians who stoked the furnaces? Jewish friends and schoolmates? Yes, but what about the good folk of Nieuwlande and Assisi who had never seen a Jew before they gave them shelter? Non-conformity? Yes, but what about the bishops and pastors, aldermen and police officers, establishment figures all, who insisted that they were holding fast to everything they had been taught and believed? A high moral code? Yes, but would you have wanted your daughter to marry Oskar Schindler?

Sources

1 Conspirators of Goodness

1. Nieuwlande: interviews with Arnold Douwes, Max Leons and Miriam Whartman.
2. Le Chambon-sur-Lignon: interviews with Pastor André Bettex, Roger May, Jean Lebrat and André Chouraqui. André Trocmé in a letter to an American friend, cited in Pierre Sauvage's article in *Moment* (October 1983). Correspondence with Lesley Maber. Philip Hallie's *Lest Innocent Blood Be Shed*. Pierre Sauvage's film, *Weapons of the Spirit*, as well as his articles in *Moment* (*op. cit.*), *The Hollywood Reporter* (17 March 1987) and a paper delivered to the Remembering for the Future conference (Oxford 1988).
3. Andonno: Albert M. Sharon's *Laissez Passer, a Different Holocaust Memoir* (by permission of Lynn Sharon).

2 The Honourable Consuls

1. Giorgio Perlasca: interview with Perlasca. Ernie Meyer's article, 'The Second Wallenberg' (*Jerusalem Post Magazine*, 29 September 1989).
2. Sempo Sugihara: interviews with Zorach Warhaftig and Michael Shilo. Warhaftig's memoirs, *Refugee and Survivor*. Articles in *Tokyo Shimbun* (17 January 1985), *Mainichi Daily News* (19 January 1985), *The Times* (London, 19 January 1985) and *Jerusalem Post* (28 and 29 November 1985 and 16 April 1991).
3. Georg Ferdinand Duckwitz: Werner David Melchior's testimony to the Eichmann trial (Jerusalem, 10 May 1961) and letter to the Israeli Foreign Ministry (26 July 1968), both in the Yad Vashem archives. Leni Yahil's *The Rescue of Danish Jewry* and a letter to Yad Vashem (1971). Interview with Richard Oestermann.
4. Aristides de Sousa Mendes: testimony by Mendes's family and Rabbi Chaim Kruger (Yad Vashem archives). Articles in *Reader's Digest* (December 1988), *Christian Science Monitor* (19 May 1967), *Los Angeles Times* (22 March 1988) and *Jerusalem Post* (23 March 1988). Interview with Dr David Shpiro.

5. Louis Haefliger: article in *Jerusalem Post* (20 May 1980).
6. Friedrich Born: Arieh Ben-Tov's *Facing the Holocaust in Budapest*. Articles in *Jerusalem Post* (24 June 1988 and 31 August 1988).

3 Prisoners' Prisoners

1. Charles Coward: John Castle's *The Password Is Courage*. Testimony by Yitzhak Perski (Yad Vashem archives). Interview with Gershon Peres (Perski).
2. Adélaïde Hautval: testimony of Adélaïde Hautval in Dering v Uris (Queen's Bench, London, 1964). *Médecine et Crimes contre l'Humanité*, testimony by Dr Hautval written in 1946 and revised in 1987 (published in 1991 by Actes Sud). Letters of Leon Uris (1964, Yad Vashem archives). *Times Law Report* (6 May 1964). Letter of Moshe Bejski (30 October 1988, Yad Vashem archives).
3. British POWs: interviews with Hannah Sara Rigler (*née* Matuson), Alan Edwards, George Hammond and Stanley Wells. Articles in *Jerusalem Post* (17 March 1989) and *Jewish Forward* (10 February 1989). BBC transcripts (Yad Vashem archives).

4 The Church Defiant

1. Erik Myrgren: interview with Myrgren. Article by Myrgren (1986, Yad Vashem archives). Survivors' testimony (Yad Vashem archives). Leonard Gross's *The Last Jews in Berlin*.
2. Gabor Sztehlo: interviews with Shmuel Ben-Dov and David Peleg. Article by Gabor Vermes, incorporating material from Sztehlo's memoirs (Gustav Adolf Kalender, 1990). Testimony of Shmuel Ben-Dov (Yad Vashem archives).
3. Archbishop Damaskinos and Anghelos Evert: testimony of Sam Modiano and Haim Cohen (Yad Vashem archives). Articles by Yitzchak Kerem (Greek Orthodox Church and Greek Police, *Computerized Encyclopedia of the Holocaust*, Wiesenthal Centre, Los Angeles). Article in *Davar* (11 June 1961).
4. Joseph André: testimony of Rachel Segal, Arieh Vishnia, Yitzhak Kubovitski, Sarah Weinberg (Yad Vashem archives). Additional material from Sylvain Brachfeld.
5. Rufino Nicacci: interview with Mirjam Ben-Horin (*née* Viterbi). Testimony of Hannah Hirsh (*née* Gelb) and Leah Halevy (*née* Baruch) (Yad Vashem archives). Article by Don Aldo Brunacci (London, *Catholic Times*, 1946). Alexander Ramati's *While the Pope Kept Silent*.
6. Anna Borkowska: Borkowska's account in *Mosty*, the magazine of Hashomer Hatzair (no. 46, Warsaw, 1948), reproduced in English in *Righteous Among Nations* by Wladyslaw Bartoszewski and Zofia Lewin.

Testimony of Abba Kovner (Yad Vashem archives), incorporating extracts from his Warsaw speech on presenting a Yad Vashem medal to Borkowska. Interview with Chaika Grossman.

5 The Benevolent Crescent

1. Mustafa Hardaga: testimony of Yosef Kabilio (Yad Vashem archives). Interviews with Binyamin Kabilio and Tovah Greenberg (*née* Kabilio). Report in *Jerusalem Post* (17 June 1985).
2. Selahattin Ulkumen: interview with Ulkumen. Report in *Jerusalem Post* (27 June 1990).
3. Refik Veseli: interviews with Gavra Mandil and Veseli.

6 An Act of Resistance

1. Ona Simaite: testimony of Abba Kovner, Sarah Nishmit and Tanya Sternthal (Yad Vashem archives). Mark Dworzecki's *Jerusalem in Rebellion and in Holocaust* (Mapai Publishers, 1948).
2. Stanislaw Dutkievicz: interview with Dutkievicz. Testimony of Stefan Grajek (Yad Vashem archives).
3. Wladislawa Choms: testimony of Brunia Roth, Ida Begeleiter and Ludmila Bogdanovich (Yad Vashem archives). Kurt R. Grossman's *Die unbesungenen Helden*.
4. Henryk Grabowski: accounts by Grabowski in *Mosty* (no. 46, Warsaw, 1948), reproduced in English in Bartoszewski and Lewin, *op. cit.*; and in Moreshet archives, Givat Havivah (1976). Testimony by Chaika Grossman (Yad Vashem archives and interview with author). Report in *Ma'ariv* (8 November 1984).
5. Leonard Glinski: interview with Glinski.
6. Witold Fomienko: testimony of Shoshana Jacobovitz (the *Book of Lutsk*, Yad Vashem archives). Interview with Mark Fomienko. Article in *Davar* (17 February 1961).
7. Joseph Jaksy: testimony of Alexander Eckstein, based on his memoirs, *We Did Fight Back*, and of Juraj Csiky and Eliyahu Arbel (all in Yad Vashem archives). Reports in *Forward*, New York (15 March 1991), and Religious News Service (8 March 1991).
8. Alexa Puti: testimony of Jacob Solomon (Yad Vashem archives).
9. Yvonne Nevejean: letters from Max Gottschalk, president of the Centre National des Hautes Études Juives, to Yad Vashem (Brussels, 1964, 1965), based on interviews with Nevejean. Articles in *Le Soir* (28 August 1987) and *Regards* (10–23 September 1987). Sylvain Brachfeld's *Ils n'ont pas eu les gosses*.
10. Alice Ferrières: testimony by Erna Stern, Solange Factor and Ruth Feldman (Yad Vashem archives).

11. Georges Dumas: testimony of Simone Ascher (*née* Nathan) and Henri Sandler (Yad Vashem archives).
12. Joszef Antall: Yad Vashem archives.
13. Halfdan Ullman: Liv Ullman (letter to author).

7 The Few Who Disobeyed

1. Hugo Armann: letter from Armann to Yad Vashem (1983). Testimony of Sara Czazkes Manishewitz and Shabtai Sternfeld (Yad Vashem archives). Report in *Jerusalem Post* (16 September 1986).
2. Anton Schmid: testimony of Shlomo Bronowski, Mordechai Tannenbaum and M. Duborzski (Yad Vashem archives).
3. Eberhard and Donata Helmrich: interview with Susi Bezalel (*née* Almann). Testimony of Sasha Weissman and Harvey Samo (Samolewitz) (Yad Vashem archives). *Jerusalem Post* interview with Cornelia Schmalz-Jacobsen (26 April 1987).
4. Roman Erich Petsche: testimony of Hava Szyk (*née* Tibor) (Yad Vashem archives) and interview with author.
5. Oskar Schindler: interview with Moshe Bejski. Schindler's account from Kurt R. Grossman, *op. cit.* (long extracts in English, *Jerusalem Post*, 29 October 1974).
6. Max Schmeling: interview with Henri Lewin. Report by Tom Tugend (*Jerusalem Post*, 26 December 1989).
7. Maria von Maltzan: testimony of Erik Myrgren and Wolfgang Hammerschmidt (Yad Vashem archives). Leonard Gross's *The Last Jews in Berlin* (*op. cit.*). Janet Watts's interview with von Maltzan (*Observer*, 15 February 1986).

Select Bibliography

Bartoszewski, Wladyslaw, and Lewin, Zofia (eds), *Righteous Among Nations: How Poles Helped the Jews* (London, Earlscourt Publications, 1969)

Ben-Tov, Arieh, *Facing the Holocaust in Budapest* (Dordrecht, Holland, Matinus Nijhoff, 1988)

Bierman, John, *Righteous Gentile: The Story of Raoul Wallenberg* (New York, Viking, 1981)

Boehm, Eric, *We Survived* (New Haven, Yale, 1949)

Borwicz, Michael, *Vies Interdites* (Tournai, Casterman, 1969)

Brachfeld, Sylvain, *Ils n'ont pas eu les gosses* (Herzliya, Institut de Recherche sur le Judaisme belge, 1989)

Castle, John, *The Password Is Courage* (London, Souvenir Press, 1954)

Dawidowicz, Lucy S., *The War Against the Jews* (New York, Holt, Rinehart and Winston, 1975)

Deutschkron, Inge, *Outcast* (New York, Fromm, 1989)

Ford, Herbert, *Flee the Captor* (Nashville, Tenn., Southern Publishing Association, 1966)

Frank, Anne, *The Diary of a Young Girl* (New York, Pocket Books, 1953)

Friedman, Philip, *Their Brothers' Keepers* (New York, Crown, 1957)

Gilbert, Martin, *The Holocaust* (London, Collins, 1986)

Gross, Leonard, *The Last Jews in Berlin* (New York, Simon & Schuster, 1982)

Grossman, Chaika, *The Underground Army* (New York, Holocaust Library, 1987)

Grossman, Kurt R., *Die unbesungenen Helden* (Berlin, Arani Verlag, 1961)

Gutman, Israel, and Zuroff, Efraim (eds), *Rescue Attempts During the Holocaust* (Jerusalem, Yad Vashem, 1974)

Gutman, Israel (ed.), *Encyclopaedia of the Holocaust* (New York, Macmillan, 1990)

Hallie, Philip, *Lest Innocent Blood be Shed* (New York, Harper & Row, 1979)

Hilberg, Raul, *The Destruction of the European Jews* (Chicago, Quadrangle, 1961)

Horbach, Michael, *Out of the Night* (London, Vallentine, Mitchell, 1967)

Keneally, Thomas, *Schindler's Ark* (UK), *Schindler's List* (US) (London, Hodder & Stoughton, 1982; New York, Simon & Schuster, 1982)

Oliner, Samuel P. and Pearl M., *The Altruistic Personality* (New York, The Free Press, 1988)

Ramati, Alexander, *While the Pope Kept Silent* (UK), *The Assisi Underground* (US) (London, Allen & Unwin, 1978; New York, Stein & Day, 1978)

Reitlinger, Gerald, *The Final Solution* (London, Vallentine, Mitchell, 1953)

Tec, Nechama, *When Light Pierced the Darkness* (New York, Oxford University Press, 1986)

Uris, Leon, *QB VII* (New York, Doubleday, 1972)

Warhaftig, Zorach, *Refugee and Survivor* (Jerusalem, Yad Vashem, 1988)

Yahil, Leni, *The Rescue of Danish Jewry* (Philadelphia, Jewish Publication Society, 1969)

Index